YOU
ARE THE
LEADER
YOU'VE BEEN WAITING FOR

ENJOYING HIGH PERFORMANCE
& HIGH FULFILLMENT AT WORK

ERIC KLEIN

You Are the Leader You've Been Waiting For,
Enjoying High Performance & High Fulfillment at Work

A Wisdom Heart Press Book
P.O. Box 232698, Encinitas, CA 92023-2698

Cataloging Information
Klein, Eric H. (Eric Harry), 1953– .
You Are the Leader You've Been Waiting For, Enjoying
High Performance & High Fulfillment at Work /
Eric Klein.

ISBN 0-9758589-4-7
1. Career Development 2. Leadership-Spiritual
3. Conduct of Life

Book Editor: Jann Einfeld
Book Designer: Lynn Fleschutz
Printed and bound by Bang Printing

Printed and bound in the United States of America.

To my sons Nathaniel and Aaron,
May you follow your true path
with clarity, courage, and compassion.

Acknowledgements

Writing a book can take over your life. I would like to thank those people who were so encouraging and supportive through this process.

To Lori Clelland for the initial edit and pruning job. You kept me going.

To Lynn Fleschutz for design brilliance and patience with my vacillating mind.

To Greg McQuerter for your guidance, coaching, and friendship.

To Carol Emerson for on-going support and keeping the pedal to the metal.

To Jann Einfeld for your gracious and elegant professionalism — and wonderful harmonies.

To Blake Anderson for walking across a challenging threshold with me. You are a model of service and vision.

To my spiritual mentor Goswami Kriyananda for teaching me the dharma in thought, word, and action.

To my wife Deborah whom I thank and acknowledge for her love, care, and insights. Your connection to truth is trustworthy. You have been a wondrous heart and soul partner for all these years. I look forward to crossing many thresholds with you in the years ahead.

CONTENTS

PREFACE

I live a few minutes walk from the Pacific Ocean. Every evening people gather on the bluff overlooking the beach to witness the sunset. As the sky changes colors and the sun nudges the horizon everyone gets very quiet. It is a threshold moment — the crossing point from day to night — and it focuses our attention. People stop moving and talking in order to be present as the sun melts into the sea. In the quiet you can hear the sound of cars speeding along the freeway a few blocks away.

Thresholds are sacred turning points that mark the place where what is ending has not yet transformed into that which is about to be. The threshold is a place of risk and possibilities. It is the place to reflect on what we have done, where we have been, as well as what calls us forward.

Most of us spend our days hurtling along like cars on the freeway, rushing from one commitment to the next. When we move this fast, we miss the opportunity that the threshold offers for personal and cultural transformation. We need to stop speeding about in order to engage a deeper level of awareness — one that is more often described in spiritual teachings than in books on work and leadership. But it is just this level of mindfulness, compassion, and depth that our work lives need in order to transform. As we touch this level of spiritual awareness it becomes obvious that our work life — indeed all of life — is our spiritual life. Everyday life and spiritual life are one and the same.

This realization is at the heart of this book. I have spent twenty years exploring how to translate this realization into practical methods that will help you thrive in your work and life. The essence of what I have learned in my own life and through working with hundreds of people is contained in this book. The ideas and practices you find in these pages have been tested in the fires of life. There is nothing more practical than spirituality when you are on the threshold of change.

This book is a conversation from my inner heart to yours. I invite you to allow my words to echo within you. As their sound fades away, you will find your own voice of truth guiding you across the threshold.

Eric Klein
Encinitas, California 2006

INTRODUCTION

*Light is an ancient symbol for consciousness and
life...Turning the lights back on — reconnecting to
the inspiration, energy, and focus that brings life
to your work — is the essential act of leadership.*

When the Lights Go Out

I was just sitting there when the lights went out. I was
working as a middle manager at a Fortune 100 company
and I had been summoned to make a presentation to a
group of senior executives. The meeting room had no
windows, walls covered with dreary gray fabric, and car-
pet that was equally bland. I was seated in one of the
molded plastic chairs lining one wall that were reserved
for visiting lower-level managers waiting to make presen-
tations. The executives sat in padded leather chairs
around a wide conference table.

As I sat there waiting, only half-listening to the
conversation that droned around the table, we were
plunged into darkness.

The company had installed motion-sensitive lights in
all the conference rooms in an effort to save money on
utility bills. This meant that the lights would go off
automatically when there was no movement in the

1

room. In this meeting, physical movement had ceased to the degree that the sensors assumed nobody was in the room. And so the lights went out.

In a sense, no one was present. There were bodies in the chairs but those bodies were so inanimate as to be undetectable by the sensors. If movement is a sign of life, then this meeting was lifeless.

Many people feel that all life has ebbed from their work. They still show up, complete the tasks, and check off the to-do list. But they have the sense that the lights, if not out, have dimmed.

Who Turns on the Light?

Light is an ancient symbol for consciousness and life. Everyday language has many reminders of the power of light. Confusion is known as *being in the dark*. When you are in a *dark mood,* you are depressed and when you are very happy, you are *radiant. Enlightenment* is associated with the highest degree of awareness and wisdom.

When the light — consciousness and vitality — of your work darkens, your sense of purpose, direction, and value dims. You may feel like you are in the dark, stumbling along, banging your knees into the furniture. Turning the lights back on — reconnecting to the inspiration, energy, and focus that brings life to your work — is the essential act of leadership.

In organizations around the world, I have met people who are waiting for a leader to come and turn on the lights — to fix things for them, inspire them, make work more meaningful and fulfilling. Great leaders, teachers, mentors, or role models can point the way but they cannot transform your work for you. You are the leader you've been waiting for. In the end it is your own choices and actions that will improve

> *You have the capacity to lead yourself to a work life of purpose and meaning.*

your work life. You have the capacity to lead yourself to a work life of purpose and meaning. You do this by awakening the authentic leader inside you.

Authentic Leadership

Authentic leadership is the pursuit of excellence (high performance) and meaning, joy, and integrity (high fulfillment). It is a path of action and reflection that brings these two factors — performance and fulfillment — together for your benefit and the benefit of the people you work with and serve. In your most purposeful and meaningful work experiences, performance and fulfillment unite:

High Performance is your power to create the work

High Performance + High Fulfillment =
Creating Desired Results with Meaning, Joy, and Integrity

---

and life you want. High Performance is about actively pursuing your goals and bringing them to fruition. The performance side of the equation engages you in the creative process of making your visions real.

High Fulfillment is your experience of meaning, joy, and integrity in the process of creating. Fulfillment is your inner experience of work. The fulfillment side of the equation attunes you to the degree of congruence between your actions and your values and guides you towards deeper levels of integrity.

Authentic leadership is determined by the depth of awareness, skill, and presence you bring to your actions and interactions.

This book is an exploration into the dynamics of high performance and high fulfillment that will provide you with principles and practices that you can use to deepen your awareness, sharpen your skills, expand your capacity to create what matters most in your work, and awaken the authentic leader inside you.

Awakening Your Leadership Potential

It is easy in the midst of constant pressures of work and unremitting change in organizations to want to stay asleep to your own leadership potential — to withdraw, disengage, or even turn cynical. It is easy but neither effective nor fulfilling.

Following the path of authentic leadership is a way of being that will transform your life. When you are on this path, you intentionally work to express your values in your daily actions. You consciously use and develop your unique gifts. You align with a deeper calling so that your personal transformation positively impacts those around you. Your own growth as an authentic leader actively enriches the world you work in.

Authentic leadership is determined neither by your position nor title, but by the depth of awareness, skill, and presence you bring to your actions and interactions. "Don't look for spectacular actions," said Mother Teresa. "What is important is the gift of yourself. It is the degree of love you insert in your deeds." This is available to each of us regardless of position or status. The leadership that is the subject of this book is a way of being. It is a way of engaging with the world from your deepest self.

I have asked many hundreds of workshop participants to recall people they admire who have positively influenced their lives personally and professionally. I ask them what they admire most about these individuals. Their answers never focus on titles or positions, but on character — on qualities like creativity, love, integrity, courage, compassion, vision, humor, spirituality, service, and wisdom. Pursuing the path of authentic leadership will transform your work by re-awakening within yourself those qualities that you see in those you most admire. These are the very qualities that will bring more light to your work.

1

SHIFT YOUR FOCUS

*Inside everyone is a great shout of joy
waiting to be born.*

David Whyte

There is something deep within you that knows what you are here to do and the direction you must move in to find your authentic work. To follow this path is to be an authentic leader. It is your birthright. You were born with unique gifts and with a sense of excitement about contributing to the world. Although somewhere along the way you may have forgotten this, you can lead yourself back to a path that will bring more passion, purpose, and meaning to your work. This can require a change of focus and a willingness to explore aspects of yourself that you may have ignored.

A story from the Sufi tradition of the wise-fool Mulla Nassruddin speaks to this shift in focus. Nassruddin is a trickster figure who offers us profound wisdom in the guise of humor and paradox. He pokes fun at conventional attitudes and invites us to wake up to our neglected potential.

The Mulla Nassruddin was discovered late one evening on his hands and knees searching intently in the road beneath a street lamp. His friend, coming

upon him in this position asked, "Mulla, what are you looking for?"
Nassruddin replied, "I am searching for my keys."
"Where did you lose them?" the friend inquired.
"Across the street," was the ready reply.
"Then why," asked the confused friend, "are you searching so intently over here?"
"Oh," explained Nassruddin, looking up, "the light here is much better."

Like Nassruddin, you may have lost something important and may be searching to:

- Deepen your sense of meaning and passion at work
- Express your true gifts and talents
- Align with a compelling purpose
- Develop relationships that support your growth

But not all searching will lead to the missing key. You have to know what you are looking for. All too often people who are dissatisfied with work look for the key to high performance and high fulfillment in external factors alone. They never cross over to the "other side of the street" to look within — where the key to transformation through authentic leadership can be found.

Where to Look

Psychologist-philosopher Ken Wilber's Integral Model suggests where to look for the keys to high performance and high fulfillment. Wilber's model is a framework that encompasses all aspects of the work experience. The basic model takes the form of a quadrant diagram. The upper quadrants represent aspects of the individual, while the lower quadrants represent aspects of groups, teams, or institutions of which the individual is a member. The two left quadrants represent the inner, intangible, subjective aspects of work and the two right-hand quadrants represent the outer, observable, objective aspects.

All four quadrants influence each other and each quadrant offers a window into a specific and important aspect of your work life.

	INNER	OUTER
INDIVIDUAL	**QUADRANT 1** **SELF** Values Purpose Meaning	**QUADRANT 2** **SKILLS** Competencies Health & Fitness Skill Development Collective
COLLECTIVE	**QUADRANT 3** **CULTURE** Relationships Power Dynamics Trust & Morale	**QUADRANT 4** **ENVIRONMENT** Structure & Systems Policies & Procedures Compensation & Measurements

Adapted from Ken Wilber

Quadrant 1/Self

This quadrant focuses on the individual/subjective aspects of your work life. You ask, "What do I value? Who am I? What am I here for?" Here you become aware of your core values, deep beliefs, and essential purpose — and reflect on how these manifest in your current work. In this quadrant you attend to your inner development, recognizing that to truly change your work there must be a change in your own consciousness.

Quadrant 2/Behavior

This quadrant shifts the focus to the individual/ external aspects of your work life. You ask, "What do I know how to do? What are my skills?" You concentrate on defining and developing competencies. You see that you must develop and sharpen your skills to lead yourself to more fulfilling work. You pay attention to gaining experiences, training, or other developmental activities that will raise your level of measurable competence so that you can produce consistently excellent results.

Quadrant 3/Culture

Here the focus is on the collective/internal aspects of your work life. You ask, "Who can I turn to for support? Who are my allies and guides?" You turn your attention to organizational culture — the interior, often hidden, dynamics of collective values, beliefs, and "unwritten rules" that affect morale and accountability. You are reminded that you can't do it alone. You need to build relationships, deepen trust, and align intentions with like-minded people in order to risk, dream, and fulfill your leadership potential.

Quadrant 4/Environment

This quadrant deals with the collective/external aspects of your work life. You ask, "What is going on out there? Where are the opportunities? What are the trends?" Here you become aware of the organizational systems and structures. You look at job openings, consider career paths, study the compensation and benefits packages. You focus on the larger world — the social, economic, regulatory, and technological systems — and consider how to navigate these to your greatest advantage.

Where to Focus

I have asked many hundreds of people where they focus their attention and activities when they want to improve their work life. Most people say their attention and energy goes to the outer-objective quadrants. They focus primarily on Quadrant 4/Environment to identify career paths, job openings, market trends, and financial opportunities. They also examine Quadrant 2/Skills to see how their competencies match the market needs.

Most people tell me, "I focus on the environment because it is the obvious thing to do. I know how to do it and what to look for. The same with my skills. Quadrants 2 and 4 are tangible and clear. I've managed my career this way for years. It's familiar."

Focusing on the known, the familiar, often means ignoring other aspects of your work life that need attention. Looking only in the familiar quadrants may not reveal important keys that can bring high performance and high fulfillment to your work. You can be like Nassruddin who spends all his time looking under the lamp post — just because the light is better.

When pressed, most people acknowledge that focusing on external factors is not enough to generate transformational change. They say that the key to change comes from within — from clarity regarding your passions, your strengths, and the contribution you most want to make. Inner knowing ignites the commitment that is necessary to sustain your focus in the face of inevitable challenges. People tell me that along with inner clarity and personal commitment, another key to change is building supportive relationships that encourage honest reflection and foster accountability.

> *The key to change comes from within.*

The missing keys to transforming your work lie in the internal, subjective quadrants. These are the places of inner work that we often ignore in our fast-paced world. There is too much at stake to keep ignoring the inner work. If you are serious about your work and want to exercise the kind of leadership that can renew it — you need to take the time to look within.

For too long the inner and the outer dimensions of work have been kept apart. We are living with the consequences of this split every day. When work is defined only by the outer quadrants, it becomes, in Wilber's terms, a flatland where the inner dimensions of work are both ignored and devalued. Only the objectively measurable factors are given weight. Quantifiable results alone are real. All else is suspect. We call this the bottom line as though there were nothing deeper than numbers. In splitting off the two left quadrants, we strip our work life of meaning, purpose, and community. The workplace becomes a flatland denuded of feeling, relationship, and passion.

The quest to improve your work life requires that you turn within to the neglected left quadrants.

Looking within means crossing the street and taking on unfamiliar inquiries. You will need to examine the connection between your daily work and your sense of life purpose. You will have to reclaim your core values and find or strengthen relationships that can provide the support and guidance to turn your inner realizations into tangible action.

Tools for the Journey

The inner work that you do alone and with supportive partners will strengthen your inner listening. You will sharpen your ability to attune to trustworthy inner guidance and to discern the difference between the voice of judgment that compares you to others and the voice of courage that asks you to embrace your uniqueness; between inherited assumptions and essential wisdom that reminds you of your own deepest knowing; between ambition and your sincere wish to make a difference in the world.

We can learn much from the spiritual traditions when it comes to this inner journey. Teachings in all traditions show how to shed outmoded ways of being in order to live more abundantly and joyfully. The exemplars of the spiritual traditions offer models of what it means to yoke inner growth with service to others. This is sorely needed in most organizations and is essential to the transformation of our work lives.

Taking this inner approach to work and leadership means accepting that *career change and personal change are inextricably linked;* that *the lever for lasting change is within your own consciousness.* It means discovering how to release yourself from self-imposed limitations and actively liberate your high performance-high fulfillment potential. The practice of meditation is ideally suited to both these ends as it develops a steadiness of attention that allows you to:

- Compassionately dissolve the patterns of thought that contain your inherent creativity
- Maintain clarity and unstrained focus in the midst of change
- Courageously embody your gifts and follow your true path

A story from the early days of aviation illustrates the need for meditative awareness. A grizzled and legendary test pilot was putting a new engine through its paces with a junior colleague.

Take-off went smoothly, but shortly into the flight the young man heard a disturbing clanging sound. He glanced nervously at the old pro, who appeared oblivious. A few minutes later the clanging returned with greater intensity. The young man yelled out, "Didn't you hear that?!" Without blinking the legendary pilot reached to the control panel and, spinning a dial, said, "In cases like that — we just turn up the radio."

The "noise" of our mind and the busy-ness of our lives tend to override the gnawing awareness that something is amiss in our work life. The ephemeral nature of high performance and high fulfillment is the by-product of a scattered mind.

Meditation

Meditation practice retrains the mind by systematically turning down the "noise" of distracting thoughts and emotions. The practice of meditation quiets the mind, opens the heart, and connects you with an uncontrived, natural inner strength. Meditation increases clarity so that you are aware of outer events and inner states without being overwhelmed or compelled by either. When situations appear threatening and inner states become overwhelming, it is almost impossible to see with clarity, respond with compassion, or act with courage and creativity. When attention is unsteady, high performance and high fulfillment are elusive.

There are hundreds of ways to practice meditation. The spiritual traditions of the world are rich repositories of methods for steadying attention, stilling thought, and expanding awareness. If you are aligned with a particular spiritual tradition — turn to the great teachers and mystics of your faith. In their teachings you will find guidelines and techniques for developing meditative attention.

Often when we begin a meditation practice, we discover the startling degree of activity within the mind. Having taken the time for stillness, we are thrown into a world of incessant thinking and emotional tension. The body can become uncomfortable as we experience the accumulated stress from living at the velocity of the to-do list. The initial encounter may be frustrating. Nothing in our education or work cultures has taught us how to work with our own minds. This is why following a time-tested method is so useful.

The traditions of meditation around the world have developed simple and skillful ways of working with our unbridled thoughts and discomforting tensions. Through the practice of meditation you learn to face your own imbalances with compassion. Rather than avoid or override disturbing thoughts, you learn to discern a level within you that is deeper than thought. You discover a place of clarity that is both open to and at the same time fundamentally undisturbed by events or the machinations of thought and emotion. You learn to remain in this effortless place of steadiness and mindfulness, which naturally supports taking appropriate and skillful actions.

Through meditation you learn to bring your attention back into balance. You do this by returning again and again to the object of meditation. The object of meditation is that symbol, sound, prayer, image, attitude, or feeling that you have chosen. Every traditional approach to meditation provides a variety of objects to focus upon. Over time the practice of returning to the object of meditation each time the mind wanders away opens you to the experience of being at full attention without tension. You discover a wakeful, alert, yet profoundly released state of awareness that is ever-present. As your practice develops, this state of alertness and openness emerges more and more in your daily life.

The key is regular practice. Begin to incorporate moments of reflective silence and meditative stillness into your schedule. Make time — even for only a few moments — to release your mind from the bustle of the day. No matter how many times the mind wanders — simply bring it back to the object of meditation. Do this with a sense of graciousness and ease as though you were placing a

Release yourself from self-imposed limitations.

rose carefully in a beautiful vase or escorting an honored guest to her seat at the head of the table. Through practice attention becomes steadier and distractions begin to drop away. As they do you are freed to experience the aliveness of the present moment.

The great American psychologist William James has written, "The faculty of voluntarily bringing back a wandering attention over and over again is the very root of judgment, character, and will. An education, which should improve this faculty, would be education par excellence." Meditation is a practical and portable way to tame your wandering attention and to enhance those qualities of character — clarity, compassion, and courage — that support high performance and high fulfillment.

Breath Awareness

Awareness of the breath is a common denominator of a variety of meditation practices from around the world. The breath is a universally honored object of meditation. In some traditions the breath is linked to sacred sounds such as mantras or prayers. In some traditions the breath is used to enliven visualizations or deepen devotion. Many sacred texts refer to the holy and profound nature of the breath, equating it with spirit and life itself. In practice, meditation on the breath is a wonderful vehicle for developing alert presence. The breath is always available as an object of meditation, whether you are in a quiet room or an active meeting — the breath is an ever-present invitation to steady your attention, let go of self-limiting thoughts, and rest in the creative potential of the present moment.

When I am coaching executives there are times when I need to challenge their assumptions and support them in seeing their problems in new ways. Many executives are not used to being questioned. They bristle at my suggestions. How I respond to their bristling is key to whether our conversation leads to breakthroughs or perpetuates the habits of the past.

I was meeting with the president of a fast growing technology company, a man with a brusque manner who was known for tearing into folks when the business hit rough spots. He had called me during one of those difficult times in order to talk about how to get his management team refocused and re-energized. As he talked I began to feel tension in the pit of my stomach and tightness in the back of my neck. I noticed that my mouth had formed into a kind of frozen smile and that I was nodding encouragingly.

The incongruity between my smile and my tight stomach was confusing. I tried to think of what I should say, but my mind was blank. I felt trapped in a conversation that was becoming less and less authentic with each nod of my head.

That is when I took a full, mindful breath and let the field of my awareness expand to include both my client and the rhythm of my breathing. With each breath my attention steadied. I could feel the tension drain from my stomach and neck. My rigid smile relaxed. And an image of my friend Richard Johnson flashed into my mind.

Big Bad Scary Dude

Richard was a yoga student who had, at one time, worked as a guard at the county prison. One evening, Richard was admitting a new inmate. Looking at the man's shaved head, tattooed muscles, and scowling expression, Richard felt his stomach clench and a little voice inside exclaim, "This is one Big, Bad, Scary Dude!"

Whenever he saw the Big Bad Scary Dude (BBSD), the hairs on the back of Richard's neck would rise. Each time he walked by the BBSD's cell, Richard would find his heart pounding and his palms glazed with sweat. Richard would have imaginary encounters with the BBSD while driving home from work. Pulling onto the freeway, he imagined the BBSD sitting in the back seat. "Hi," the BBSD would say. "How did you get in here?" Richard would think, his shoulders hunched, his grip tightening on the steering wheel. There he was out on the freeway doing seventy, yet inside himself he felt frozen, paralyzed, unable to think, barely breathing.

Richard overcame his BBSD one afternoon while watching the inmates exercising. "The longer I watched, the more my back hurt," Richard told me. "I started thinking that it would feel really good to do a few yoga postures. Then I thought — no, this might not be the best place to do yoga."

Richard's body began willing itself into a yoga posture. He went with it. He felt the tension in his back release. At that moment, a voice boomed from across the yard, "Triangle Pose!!"

Richard snapped to a standing position. As his eyes scanned the yard for the source of the sound, Richard saw the BBSD smiling broadly stretched in triangle pose. As their eyes met,

I have learned over the years that the most creative and trustworthy actions come from meditative awareness.

the BBSD stood, brought his palms together in a traditional greeting of peace, nodding slowly. "At that moment," Richard remembered, "the bars in my mind dissolved away. I saw past the BBSD label. I looked through that scowl to his soul."

As I sat with my client and felt my breath, the bars in my own mind dissolved. I saw how I had over-reacted to his gruff demeanor — by becoming tense, smiling, and paralyzed. I felt compassion for my reaction. I saw the ways in which my client was afraid and struggling underneath his rough exterior. I felt his vulnerability.

Centered on the breath, I saw and felt this all without judgment or commentary.

"This must be a scary time for you," I suggested. My client paused. He swallowed and sighed. Our conversation shifted gears as he began to tell me about his fears and the ways in which he struggled to stay in control.

I have learned over the years that the most creative and trustworthy actions come from meditative awareness. Through ongoing practice one learns to dissolve the self-limiting habits of reaction into the breath. Meditation is a practice that teaches you to let go of constriction and discover the natural sense of inner support and strength that is there in each moment. As our experience deepens, our trust in our own awareness grows and we enter into each moment with greater clarity, compassion, and courage.

Learning Partners

Along with the practice of meditation, I recommend that you find two learning partners to support you on this journey to high performance and high fulfillment. Ideally they will be on a similar journey and will be reading this book as well. This trio of fellow travelers will be able to remind each other to stay on track, and support each other in the often difficult work of reconnecting to our potential for high performance and high fulfillment.

In the midst of unrelenting pressure it is rare to take time to build the kind of relationships that reinforce your sense of purpose and passion. But along with meditation, meeting with your learning partners is key to sustaining developmental momentum. Learning partners support each other to live purposefully and authentically in the midst of organizational life, rife as it is with uncertainty, impermanence, and surprise.

Meeting with your learning partners is a practice that supports you in creating what matters most in your work life. If you wait for such a meeting time to appear... it never will. The irony is that on the one hand you and your learning partners are so busy that you really need each other's support. And on the other hand you and they don't have time for anything else in your schedules. As with meditation practice, you will need to make the commitment to devote time, which may be an opportunity to say "no" to other less important demands.

Learning partners are not advice givers, givers of action plans, nor problem solvers. To be a learning partner means to listen with clarity and compassion; and to encourage your partners to listen within themselves with clarity and compassion. It also means to encourage them to courageously awaken to their own possibilities.

When you are being a learning partner your core task is to support another person in their learning in whatever way you can without doing the learning for them. You want them to learn to fish for themselves, not to depend on you or others to fish for them.

There will be a strong temptation to give your partner answers, advice, to solve a problem for them, to spare them the struggle, sweat, and tears. This is what makes being a learning partner so transformational. If you go into rescue mode when your partner is stuck, confused, suffering, you are telling them — by your actions — "I know you don't have it in you to work this through. I know that you need my wisdom to guide you through the dark." You will be reinforcing their doubts and fears even while appearing to be helpful.

Instead of saving the day — pause, release the tensions that are pushing you to rescue them and connect to your breath. Affirm to yourself that they have the resources they need to work their way through the issues they face. Your job is to stay connected to a place of balance within yourself and support them in listening to their inner guidance. You do this by listening deeply.

The way you listen creates an environment in which your partner can freely explore their inner guidance. While listening it may seem like you aren't doing much. Don't be fooled. As your listening deepens, you will be silently inviting your partner to go deeper and listen to the promptings of his or her inner guidance.

Listening is a kind of meditation. To listen deeply, allow your body to be alert and relaxed. Do a quick body check — shoulders, neck, back. Notice if you are holding your breath. You will listen more easily as your breath finds a full, natural rhythm. Soften your eyes. Listen as you would to a bird singing in

All you have to do is help them hear the voice of their deeper wisdom.

a tree, the sound of the ocean, or a stream rushing by. In other words, drop your agenda. Drop what you think they need. Drop your solutions for their problems and open.

If you feel the urge to demonstrate your insightfulness or creative problem-solving abilities — take a breath and refocus. Instead of fire-fighting problems with answers and reactive solutions, take time to listen deeply. Endure the discomfort of withholding advice or resolving the tension you feel. Breathe. Reaffirm the belief that your learning partner has the capabilities to succeed, learn, and choose the next steps. As a listener all you have to do is help him or her hear the voice of their deeper wisdom.

Selecting Your Learning Partners

Selecting your learning partners is based more on intuition than analysis. When you ask yourself, "Whom do I want as learning partners?" — notice the faces that flash instantly to mind. You may have someone in your life with whom you already have an unstructured learning partnership, you support each other and talk about your hopes and dreams. Whomever you choose, the person should be someone that:

You trust

Your learning partner should be someone that you can open up to and feel comfortable talking with about your hopes, dreams, and doubts. Thinking about being vulnerable may give you butterflies in the stomach. That's natural and it is just an indication that you are stepping into new territory. On the other hand, if thinking about your learning partner sets off alarms, pause. Check in with yourself. Do you feel that this person will both support and challenge you to work more fully and more creatively?

You believe in

You should sense great possibilities in your learning partner. You see that they have untapped possibilities

A Simple Practice of Stillness

• *Sit with a straight spine and let go of tension. Sit on the floor or use a chair with a straight back. When seated on the floor, elevate your body on a firm cushion or folded blanket to reduce strain on the back. Experiment with cushions of different heights to find a comfortable position. Keep your spine straight but not stiff.*

• *Focus your mind on your breath. Watch and feel the rise and fall of your abdomen. Feel the passage of your breath in and out of your nasal passages.*

• *Take several deep diaphragmatic breaths. Place your hands on your belly and feel the expansion as you inhale, the relaxation and subtle contraction as you exhale. For several breaths extend and deepen the breathing. Use the diaphragm in a conscious yet relaxed way. Then let the breath return to its own natural rhythm.*

• *Maintain a still and relaxed posture as you focus your complete attention on the incoming and outgoing breath. If thoughts or sensations arise, simply dissolve them into the breath. Return to the breath. Put your full mind on the natural rhythmic pattern of your breath.*

• *When your mind and body have quieted, let go of any particular concentration and just sense the quality of stillness. You may feel it in your heart or sense it as an all-encompassing spaciousness. The stillness can include the sounds of the environment around you. Don't try to define it. Just experience it. Bathe in the stillness.*

and unexpressed gifts. You know they are great as they are and that that they have more to give, more to be.

You can communicate with regularly

You have to be able to meet, either in person or by phone at least once a month. Without regular communication, the process bogs down. It takes contact to keep the fire burning.

Is committed to the process

Your learning partner needs to understand what they are getting into. Review this section of the book together. Talk about your individual goals. Make sure that you both want to do this with equal intensity. Uninterrupted time is essential for building the kind of focus, openness, and sensitivity that will yield the greatest learning and produce the most potent action.

Will preserve confidentiality

Confidentiality creates a safe place for exploring and learning. It creates a sacred container that protects the process.

The focus of learning partnering is to:
- Deepen your learning about what it means to create high performance and high fulfillment
- Take actions to express your values, develop your gifts, and follow your calling

This means that accountability is central to the process. Accountability makes the learning partnering process focused and disciplined. In learning partnerships, accountability has nothing to do with judgment or blame. Accountability in this context is about telling the truth and learning from your actions. With this in mind, it is easy to see how we can learn as much from a so-called failure as from an accomplishment.

Meeting with Your Learning Partners

The learning partnership is about high performance and high fulfillment. In the end, this comes down to the practical tasks of making appointments, reading the book, doing the practices, and following the process. Here is the standard agenda for a meeting:

• *5 minutes – Opening Process: This might include a short reading that one of you brings, a moment of silence to focus on your breath, or whatever else will allow you all to step away from the pressures of the day and focus on the session.*

• *45 minutes – "On air": Reports, Learnings, Future Actions: Each learning partner gets 15 minutes to be "on air."*

• *5 minutes – Closing Process: How's it working?*

When you are "on air," the time is wholly yours. The focus is you, your learning, the challenges you are facing, the successes you are having, and the questions that are arising. It is up to you to let your learning partners know how you want to use the time.

Usually, you'll use the time to bring your learning partners up to date on your journey to high performance and high fulfillment. You will share new issues or challenges that you want to clarify and act upon.

Meeting Guidelines

Here are some suggested guidelines:

• *Start from where you are.* *Don't treat this like any other status report. Focus on what matters.*

• *Maintain an open attitude to the questions and responses of your learning partner.* *You are in the learning role. If your learning partner says something that bothers you — focus more on your reaction than their behavior. Use your reaction to dig more deeply into what matters most to you. Keep the focus on your development — not your learning partner's skill.*

• *Focus on your development.* *Talk about your experience, your feelings, and your thoughts. Minimize analyzing other people, their motives, and their personalities. Talking about how others need to change takes you off track.*

• *Be as vulnerable as you're comfortable with. Experiment with sharing your thoughts and feelings.* *Use the learning partnering process to "think out loud." Your learning partners are there to support your exploration. So the more you disclose, the more you will learn and the better choices you will make.*

• *Ask for what you need.* *This is your time to get the kind of support that will be useful. Help your learning partner learn how to give you the kind of support that will move you forward. Let your learning partner know what is helpful and what you need.*

2

BEGIN HERE AND NOW

*Initiatory events are those that define who a
person is, or cause some power to erupt from
them, or strip everything from them until all that
is left is their essential self.*

Michael Meade

Establishing a regular meditation practice and meeting
with learning partners will naturally support the
transforming of your work. You don't have to make an
extravagant gesture or go on a grueling trek to reach the
place where you can begin to make deep changes.
The entry to transformation is within an arm's length — at
your next meeting or in your next conversation. "Wherever
you are is the entry point," writes the poet Kabir.

Pushes and Pulls

Several years ago, my wife and I led a meditation
retreat on the island of Maui. We brought our sons,
Aaron and Nathaniel, then ages 3 and 13. While we were
teaching they roamed the vast property, gathering
papayas, stones, and insects. One afternoon, I took
Nathaniel, a budding surfer, to a local beach break.
After four days of baby-sitting his younger brother,

Nathaniel was ready to surf. As soon as I parked the car, he was out the door, surfboard tucked under his arm, charging out of sight over the dunes to the beach. I walked slowly up the dunes, enjoying the sunlight filtering through the palms. When I got to the top of the dunes and looked at the surf my heart stopped. The waves were huge. They crashed mercilessly in explosions of white water.

I began running towards the water looking for my son. I spotted him ducking under a towering wave. The wave thundered as it broke. Nathaniel resurfaced on the other side and kept paddling. I began shouting into the wind, "Be careful. Be careful." I was running back and forth at the water's edge — screaming warnings, "Watch out!! Duck!!" and pleading, "Don't go too far out!" He couldn't hear a thing. The sound of my voice was blown to pieces by the wind.

There is a part of you that may be like Nathaniel — ready to take the plunge and prepared for the challenge of changing who you are and how you work. And there may be a part of you that is more like me — fearful, nervous, running back and forth on the shore shouting warnings into the wind. The urge within you to be authentic, to make a contribution, and to grow can be in conflict with the urge to play it safe.

Feel the Burn

Leading yourself to high performance and high fulfillment can place you in a dilemma. You can feel the underlying tension inside where your old definitions of success are in conflict with the wish to experience high performance and high fulfillment.

Being in this dilemma generates heat. There is palpable tension. This is an inner crisis in which, C.G. Jung tells us, "You are called to die to the old self...and liberate the new man or woman within." How you work with this tension is central to your success in taking your work to a new level. People tend to pull back from the intensity so as not to be burned by the fire.

The fire is there to teach you, purify you, and transform you.

But the fire is there to teach you, purify you, and transform you. The characteristics of authentic leadership are forged in that fire. What is burned is that which no longer serves you or contributes to your high performance and high fulfillment. Freed are the deeper parts of who you are — the authentic leader within.

This journey of transformation will carry you to deeper levels of self-awareness and creativity. In the words of Ken Wilber, you will "transcend and include" what has gone before at each level of growth. You transcend the limitations of your old beliefs about what you can create and the old models about what work means to you. And you include the talents, knowledge, values, and experiences that can continue to enrich you and your world. The trajectory of authentic leadership is towards richer more powerful ways of being in the world to create and serve with integrity and joy.

You've Been There Before

We have all had times of wholeness, integrity, courage, and creativity when we have glimpsed our own capacity to create purposeful and meaningful work. You've probably experienced the satisfaction of pursuing a deeply held vision and experienced what it means to be purified by that inner fire that reconfigures and strengthens you. In those times you experienced the fusion of high performance and high fulfillment — where awareness, skill, and devotion to a noble goal turned into actions that enrich you and your world.

In those peak experiences lie the clues to your unique high performance-high fulfillment equation. Learning to listen to those clues in your life experiences helps you identify what it takes for you to bring your work alive. There are messages within your experiences that can go unheard if you do not pause and listen. Educator and author Parker Palmer points out that, "Before I can tell my life what I want to do with it, I must listen to my life telling me who I am."

There are messages within your experiences that can go unheard if you do not pause and listen.

Start with the high points of your work history — the times when high performance and high fulfillment came together offer a profound glimpse into what authentic leadership looks like for you. These experiences are a reminder, as poet Mark Nepo writes, that "joy in what you do is not an added feature, it is a sign of deep health."

Kid-Run Carnival

One of my earliest experiences of high performance and high fulfillment occurred in 1964 when I was eleven years old. I grew up in Manhattan but spent the summers at a beach house on Fire Island. Summers on Fire Island were paradisiacal for a kid from the city. On Fire Island there were no cars. I ran barefoot all summer.

Many places on Fire Island had no sidewalks. Miles of boardwalks rose and fell along the contours of the sand dunes. A particular stretch of boardwalk was called the roller coaster. Perched on our banana seat bikes at the top of the roller coaster, my friend Victor Smallburg and I got our big idea. We decided to put on Fire Island's first kid carnival.

Every year on Fire Island at the end of the summer the Fire Department put on a fund-raising carnival. Designed as a casino night, kids weren't allowed to participate. So we decided to put on a carnival just for kids in the backyard at Victor's house.

As we sat on the boardwalk, we started dreaming about what would be in the carnival. We imagined a balance beam — a 2x4 slung between two cinder blocks; a test of strength — two buckets of wet sand with a broom handle tied between them; and a blindfolded wagon ride. We'd have beanbag tosses, dart throws, a raffle, and a gypsy fortuneteller.

The idea seemed irresistible. Three of our friends immediately joined in — Josh Touster, Adam Feldman, and Tommy Farber. It took two days of negotiating to convince a girl in the neighborhood, Jackie Frank, to play the part of the gypsy fortuneteller. Within a week and a half the events were built. We stapled announcements to every telephone pole within bike riding distance.

On the appointed Saturday we got up extra early and sat in Victor's backyard waiting. Families came from all over the island. Teenagers brought their younger brothers and sisters. We were overrun with people. And it was a blast. Photographers from the local newspaper, The Fire Island News, came and took photos and interviewed Victor and me about our big idea.

In It and Above It at the Same Time

In the late afternoon, I remember climbing the stairs to the rooftop deck and looking down on the crowd. From that vantage point I could see strangers and people I knew well moving about the yard. The sound of their voices melded into a bubbling hum. At the same time I felt enveloped in a bubble of silence. I felt both a part of the carnival and apart from it. I was aware of bringing all this about as well as being the recipient of the experience.

As I perched on the rooftop deck appreciating the activities of the carnival, there was something within me watching with detached appreciation — the people below and my own thoughts and feelings of success. It was as though all of the sound and movement in the yard and all the thoughts and feelings in my mind were contained, held, known by a wider and deeper awareness. Sitting on that rooftop deck a quality of awareness arose within me that I learned later is what the spiritual traditions refer to as "being in the world but not of it."

There is something sacred in all high performance and high fulfillment experiences. It is as though a veil is pulled back and for an instant the fabric of your moment-to-moment existence is woven with threads of wonder. The commonplace becomes saturated with meaning. "There is a depth in those brief moments which constrain us to ascribe more reality to them than all other experiences," writes the great American philosopher, Ralph Waldo Emerson.

When the carnival was over and the crowds were finally gone, Victor and I sat with bottles of Orange Crush and a shoebox filled with change and marveled at what we had created. Over the years, I have

> *There is something sacred in all high performance and high fulfillment experiences.*

spoken with hundreds of people about their times of high performance and high fulfillment. The details of the stories vary enormously. Some take place on the battlefield, others in silence. Some involve crowds, others just one person. However, they all tell the story of our tremendous capacity to make a vision real and to experience growth and meaning in the process.

Reflection & Dialogue: Recalling High Performance & High Fulfillment

Personal Reflection

What are your memories of high performance and high fulfillment? Whether these events occurred when you were eleven years old or last week, these experiences can teach you about what it means to lead yourself to a new level of impact and meaning at work. There are valuable clues in your high performance-high fulfillment stories that reveal the contour and texture of what it means for you to exercise authentic leadership.

• Recall two or three times in your work and/or life when you were most energized, engaged, and fulfilled.

• What key factors made these experiences so energizing and engaging?

• What did these experiences call forth from you?

Learning Partner Dialogue

Take turns sharing a story of high performance and high fulfillment with your learning partners. Listen and give each other feedback on what the story revealed about the person's passions, values, and natural way of leadership.

3

GO BEYOND YOUR MINDSET

In order to allow ourselves to be creative, we have
to relinquish control and overcome fear.
Why? Because creativity is life-altering.
It's a matter of seeing everything —
even when you want to shut your eyes.

Madeleine L'Engle

Look Deeply

For most of us high performance and high fulfillment experiences are transitory. They are unique, precious, and fleeting. You may even remember such times wistfully but quickly brush the memories aside as unrealistic given the pressures, pace, and demands of your current circumstances. You might even wonder, "If I have this high performance-high fulfillment capacity that is so powerful and satisfying, how come there is so much struggle, confusion, and cynicism in my daily work life?"

How You Lost Touch

It is easy to become so absorbed in the content of your work — the tasks, the dramas, the situations — that you forget to stay centered and connected to your own high performance and high fulfillment equation.

Take a look around. A thousand things capture and fragment your attention. You are plagued by what meditative traditions call the monkey mind. They compare your everyday working mind to an agitated monkey — leaping constantly from branch to branch — from thought to thought, from stimulus to stimulus. With no enduring sense of direction, purpose, or meaning, with no inner guidance or inspiration, the mind gets lost in an endless sequence of events.

The culture that surrounds us at work keeps the monkey mind in motion — the to-do lists run on and on; new demands, expectations, and enticements pop up around every corner. Living in this scattered state can disable your capacity to call forth your inner resources to meet situations creatively.

Pulling Your Boat to the Shore

An ancient teaching compares your plight to that of a person in a rowboat. Having thrown the boat's anchor into the sand of a nearby island, he begins pulling intensely hand over hand on the rope. In this image the anchor stands for your mind, the thoughts and beliefs you have about your work, and your own leadership potential for transforming that work into something more.

Your everyday mindset is an ingrained combination of beliefs, assumptions, and generalizations that operate invisibly or unconsciously. Your mindset drives what you do and how you do it. You are anchored to your mindset and it in turn anchors you to a limited and repetitive series of experiences. Have you noticed how you seem to encounter the same challenges and the same obstacles at work over and over again? You may feel like you are on a treadmill that keeps bringing you back to familiar frustrations again and again.

In a moment of lucidity, you might pause, look around your workplace and wonder how you got there. The teaching of the rowboat, the anchor,

> *Your mindset drives what you do and how you do it.*

and the island suggests that you pulled yourself to the shore of whatever island you are on. You anchor yourself to experiences that reflect your underlying mindset.

Your mindset is like an inner guidance system. If you have the mindset that "work is a struggle," your inner guidance system will anchor you to a set of experiences that reflect and reinforce this view. Your workplace experiences, the people you meet, and the interactions you have will tend to reinforce your belief that work is a struggle.

An alternative mindset perceives work as "joyful service." In that mindset, your inner guidance system will anchor you to a set of experiences and interactions that will tend to reinforce the belief that work is a place where you experience joy and satisfaction.

Structured unconsciously, your inner guidance system is operating automatically. You are being guided by a mindset that may not take you towards high performance and high fulfillment. Fortunately you can free yourself from the limitations of your own beliefs and assumptions and can pull up anchor, set a new direction, and recalibrate your inner guidance system to steer you to the islands of high performance and high fulfillment.

Go Beyond Your Mindset

This process of freeing yourself from an old mindset in order to adopt a new more expansive mind was called metanoia in ancient Greece. The term *meta* suggests this change is one of moving beyond or outside of accustomed limits. *Noia* refers to mind and conditioned way of knowing. This process of inner change, which initiates the transformation of your work, requires a new way of thinking about and understanding what it means to lead and work. It requires a new thought system that can take you beyond what is possible using the old mindset.

As you loosen the anchor of your old views, you will begin to reconsider your work. You will be aware of the need to refocus and renew. You will begin to wonder about options for change or about what you can do to reignite your sense of enthusiasm and purpose.

The liberating point to remember is that the source of high performance and high fulfillment is not other people. Your colleagues, bosses, parents and family, do not define your leadership. Your responses to life are self-generated and therefore can be self-regenerated. You can enhance your level of performance and fulfillment by reshaping the patterns of your mind.

The first step to reshaping patterns in your mind is

to identify your mindset relating to your work. The performance and fulfillment aspects of work interact to produce four main mindsets. Each of these causes us to see the world and interact with others in a particular way. Each mindset is based on assumptions about what is possible and meaningful in work and life.

High Performance & Low Fulfillment: The Burnout Mindset

This is the mindset of the go-getters — the energizer bunnies of the world who are often lauded in the business press, success manuals, and leadership books. People in this mindset focus on performance while they devalue the dimension of fulfillment.

High performance is seductive. Equating success with performance unleashes a torrent of adrenaline. Running on high-octane fuel keeps you moving forward. There is no time for reflection here. Only forward momentum counts. What matters is production, outcomes, making it happen. In this world the bottom line is the only real measure of worth. To talk of fulfillment is to be soft, or worse — touchy feely.

This mindset does produce results, but when you stop between meetings or tasks to take a breath, you can experience a hollowness beneath the hubbub. There is lots of action but little meaning. You are meeting or exceeding expectations, but your sense of purpose is out of focus and your joy is diminished. Driving home, you may remember that your real gifts, your unique talents, are going untapped.

Some people hold on to this mindset for years. They find it stimulating to break through barriers and bring projects to completion. Entire organizations can be anchored in this mindset. Organizations are littered with very successful, spiritually impoverished people. These people seldom notice that their lives are impoverished because the single-minded focus on performance is so seductive. In such environments being busy is a badge of honor. When you ask people how they are, they groan (while simultaneously gloating) "I'm sooo busy!" Busy-ness equals worthiness. The speed at which one moves reveals one's importance. Multi-tasking over lunch is considered virtuous.

The theme music for this mindset is any composition with a driving beat and a screaming horn section — the Rocky theme or the William Tell Overture. This is the attitude of the action hero or heroine who takes on all challenges, leads the charge, and exerts amazing efforts — all as evidence of his or her irreplaceable value.

Life hurtles along at an ever-accelerating tempo. Slowing down opens up room for reflection, which can connect you with your own dissatisfaction. This mindset discourages self reflection; it discourages your focusing on where you are headed and if that is your desired destination. Those around you may try to get your attention. If you are fully entrenched in this mindset, any suggestions to slow down will sound like attempts to derail or destroy you. The more successful you become, the more you feel you have to lose by pausing to examine your motives and purpose. Often people do

FULFILLMENT

	LOW	HIGH
HIGH	BURNOUT	AUTHENTIC LEADER
LOW	VICTIM	LOTUS EATER

PERFORMANCE

not question the high performance-low fulfillment mindset, as they become swept up in it themselves, consumed by staying on task, keeping up, and meeting deadlines. Conversations revolve around projects, plans, and programs.

Operating from this mindset for an extended time leads to burn out. Poet David Whyte captures the experience of burnout in his poem "Sweet Darkness" when he writes, "When your eyes are tired, the world is tired also. When your vision has gone, no part of the world can find you." Ignoring the fulfillment dimension is like burning the bridge that connects you to your soul, your values, your deeper purpose. The sheer weight of your multi-tasked identity becomes too much. Your shoulders collapse and even your ability to perform begins to wear away.

Low Performance & High Fulfillment: The Lotus Eater Mindset

The opposite of the go-go action hero is the mindset of low performance and high fulfillment. Here the focus shifts from producing results to having fun. This mindset is named for the Lotus Eaters described in Homer's *Odyssey*. In the tale, Ulysses and his men are headed home for Ithaca when a strong north wind blows them off course to the land of the Lotus Eaters.

At first the Lotus Eaters seem friendly and entertaining. They give Ulysses' men some of their food — the lotus root — to eat. As a result of ingesting this food, the sailors lose all interest in returning home, preferring to languish in the indolent comfort of the Lotus Eaters' company.

This mindset is less common in organizations, although the lapses of attention and spacing out that punctuate many meetings are reminiscent of the Lotus Eaters' state of unconsciousness. The Lotus Eater mindset considers exercising leadership and wonders, "Why bother?" Within this framework, you cannot get motivated to chase after rewards; they seem pointless. Your attention shifts to keeping yourself happy. You believe you have seen through the rat race after having taken a few laps around the track with the blisters to prove it. You conclude that the effort isn't worth it, that it makes more sense to take it easy. You give up on winning and lose touch with both the drive to act and your inner purpose.

You equate fulfillment with relaxation. This mindset reasons that if you aren't exerting yourself, you're fulfilled. You want satisfaction without struggle or strain. You aspire to a perpetual spa-lifestyle where the challenges of living are handled by others, the pace is slowed down, and the background music is a pacifying drone. As far as you can see, there is nothing to get excited about.

You no longer manage your time, but look for ways to stay entertained. In the workplace this means taking breaks, discussing last night's reality T.V. show, and using the comput-er to play games or email jokes to friends. One manager in an organization I worked with spent the major portion of each day combing through a stack of periodicals clipping and cataloging amusing cartoons for use in his presen-tations. He had a library of cartoons sorted by topic. He chuckled his way through the morning while his staff took up the slack.

The Lotus Eater's diet of distractions does not provide the minimum daily requirements that nourish the soul.

Initially, this mindset feels enjoyable. But like the burnout pattern, it is missing something essential. The Lotus Eater's diet of distractions does not provide the minimum daily requirements that nourish the soul. A vacuum of meaning develops that insidiously drains the vitality from your being. Without engagement in work, without the creative tension of bringing visions into reality, the muscles that power your leadership grow flaccid.

You need to contribute, to stretch yourself and use and develop your gifts in response to everyday challenges. By giving up on the performance dimension of leadership, your experience of integrity is undermined. You are bored. The real joy of life is replaced with a manufactured laugh track. You sacrifice what you want most for what you want at the moment. You don't burn the bridge to your soul. You just wander away into a forest of confusion. Lost from your soul, you lose the capacity to care deeply, to be committed, dedicated, and enthusiastic. These attributes come from your connection to purpose. When that connection is missing, your energy begins to flatline.

> When your connection to purpose is missing, your energy beings to flatline.

Having relinquished your leadership responsibility to enrich the world through conscious effort, you are left empty handed. Except for the T.V. remote. So you spend your time clicking endlessly through the channels of your experience searching for some sign of life.

The Battle that Can't Be Won

Following the paths to burnout or the way of the Lotus Eaters diminishes your creativity and your joy. Performance without fulfillment leads to exhaustion, which inevitably erodes the will to act and undermines the joy of life. Seeking personal fulfillment induces a temporary emotional high, a short-lived buzz that gives no real satisfaction as it is ungrounded in the realities and challenges of life.

Having tasted the acrid flavor of burnout and the

empty calories of lotus-eating, you can no longer be seduced by either one. It is as though you are standing in the middle of the field of your mind, on one side hearing the strenuous and demanding voice of burnout promising that with just more effort, discipline, action — you will find fulfillment. On the other side the languid voice of the Lotus Eater offers promises of perpetual ease and satisfying indolence.

Neither extreme offers what you seek. Neither provides access to peace, direction, focus, or energy that transforms you or your world. Lost between these two poles of dissatisfaction, the monkey mind gives up.

This release from the pull of hyper-activity on the one side and entertaining lethargy on the other, brings you to a choice point at which two new paths open up. No longer dancing to the accelerated tempo of the burnout and no longer enticed by the vision of the Lotus Eater, you are turned back to yourself. You become aware again of what matters most to you. You either embrace this awareness and let it guide you on the uncharted path of authentic leadership, or you follow the last temptation of the monkey mind, and give up, opting for despair and victimhood.

Low Performance & Low Fulfillment: The Victim Mindset

If you adopt the victim mindset you give up action and you do not experience meaning in your life. You lose confidence in the future and regret the past. Instead of discovering richness in the present moment, you feel trapped. Your world narrows. You circle your emotional wagons and hunker down, hoping to be left alone. You rewrite history casting yourself as the tragic central character in a story of betrayal and disappointment.

The victim mindset is insidious, subtly coloring your world with helplessness. This mind is shrewd and has an answer for everything. The confining logic of victimization cuts off all options for responsibility and change. The victim story gives solace and reassurance that you are right and "they" are wrong. Being right becomes a substitute for meaning. You chant the mantra, "It's not my fault," until it seems that even the weather is against you. You're sure that it really is raining on your parade and on no one else's. You take everything personally and lose the connection to your deepest self.

These three mindsets — burnout, Lotus Eater, and victim — are not structured to bring meaning, joy, or purpose to your work. They are self-defeating designs. In the grip of these mindsets work becomes more and more predictable, more and more robotic. Driven by the momentum of the past, those same choices are repeated today. This creates a pattern of living and working that carries you more and more automatically through time.

When you operate with these mindsets, nothing fundamentally changes despite your efforts to make improvements. When all of your strategies are structured by these self-limiting mindsets, your efforts are like rearranging the furniture in a room — but never leaving the room. Think about your friends, family, and colleagues. How many have left an unhappy work situation, only to find themselves in the very same predicament — albeit at a new company or with a new title? The Buddha said: "What you are today is a result of all that you have thought." Your present work conditions are the visible effects of your past thoughts.

High Performance & High Fulfillment: Authentic Leader Mindset

To create high performance and high fulfillment requires that you let go of your past framework and adopt a new mindset from which new thoughts, solutions, and strategies flow. Designed to support high performance and high fulfillment, this new mindset offers you a way of being that leads to meaning, purpose, and creativity at work. The high performance-high fulfillment mindset empowers you to make choices and changes in your work from being clear on who you are, what you care about, what you want, and what the world around you needs.

This mindset combines reflective self-inquiry with keen attention to the world around you. There is an integrated focus here on action and reflection. You are motivated to act and achieve. But this motivation is not the driven impetus of the burnout mindset. You commit to action in order to realize a vision, fulfill your purpose, grow in joy, and serve others.

Several decades ago, a friend of mine went to see a renowned meditation teacher. He asked the sage, "How can I attain enlightenment?" The teacher replied, "Well, now, if you'll tell me what you mean by enlightenment,

I'll do my best to tell you how you can get it." The student said that he wanted to get to a place where he had absolutely no problems. "That's not enlightenment, that's death," retorted the sage.

By choosing high performance and high fulfillment, you won't recoil from life's problems and complexity like the Lotus Eater. Challenges are the raw materials that you use to craft a life of wholeness and meaning. The unfinished and broken nature of the workplace is where you find your path to authentic leadership. The nature of high performance and high fulfillment is such that through contributing to the world you become whole.

You are actively engaged in both realizing a vision and becoming more and more integrated as a human being. You see how your own transformation and the transformation of those around you are profoundly intertwined. It becomes your leadership responsibility to live with more awareness and integrity. As an authentic leader, you experience the joy of fulfilling your purpose moment by moment in the ordinary actions and interactions of the day.

Your Authentic Voice

At a concert by the great blues guitarist and singer Keb Mo' the program notes revealed that he had not always played music that was rooted in country blues traditions. He had tried a lot of musical styles and had some successes, but never really hit his stride until he stopped and settled back into the music that was already in him. Now, he is just himself. No posturing or contorting in an attempt to make a hit. Just the joy of honing and sharing his gifts. The joy is contagious. It fills the room. Everyone in the concert hall gets a little happier when Keb Mo' plays.

That's how authentic leadership works. When one person in the room finds their authentic voice — it makes it possible for others to remember the voice in them that seeks expression. When one person in a room abandons posturing — it makes it possible for others to be more truthful. When you move towards authentically expressing your values and using your gifts, you bring more freedom into the world.

Reflection & Dialogue: The Mindsets

Personal Reflection

Consider particularly the unskillful mindsets of burnout, Lotus Eater, and victim:

- Which of these is most familiar to you?
- What do you do when you are in this familiar mindset? How do you feel?
- What helps to get you out of these unskillful mindsets?

Learning Partner Dialogue

Ask your learning partner when and how they have experienced you in either the burnout, Lotus Eater, or victim mindsets. Discuss together how you can help each other avoid (or get out of) the burnout, Lotus Eater or victim mindsets.

4

RESETTING YOUR INNER GUIDANCE

Listen. Make a way for yourself inside yourself.
Stop looking in the other way of looking.
You already have the precious mixture
that will make you well. Use it.

Rumi

There are no roadmaps to follow to high performance and high fulfillment. You get there by resetting the direction of your inner guidance system to focus on three essential elements:

- Core Values — those deep motivators that are the source of your passion and purpose
- True Gifts — those talents and abilities that are your unique expression of greatness
- Calling — that which you most want to create through your work

These three elements orient your inner guidance system toward authentic leadership and provide you with a living compass for navigating change, making choices, and taking action in your work. When your values, gifts, and calling operate in unison your work has a sense of inner congruence and outer effectiveness. You are clear about who you are and enjoy the ways in which you bring your gifts to life through your work.

Dharma

In the ancient language of Sanskrit there is a term that wonderfully captures what it means to work in this way — to embody core values, use innate gifts, and act in alignment with essential purpose. That word is dharma.

Dharma is the essential function or nature of a person or thing. The ancient texts teach that the dharma or essential function of water is to quench thirst. Imagine a glass of water whose contents look like water, taste like water, feel and smell like water. Imagine a liquid that is like water in every way except one — it cannot quench thirst. This would be water with its dharma removed.

You have a dharma — an essential function and nature. It is your authentic leader "fingerprint" composed of your core values, a unique combination of innate gifts, and a calling that is yours to follow and fulfill. Your dharma is as unique as your fingerprint. It is a deep and individual design that contains the secrets of what it means for you to live truthfully.

To work in accord with your dharma is to fully and actively realize your leadership destiny. Whether your dharma is fulfilled is up to you. No one can live your values for you, express and develop your gifts, or pursue your calling. This is your work alone — your dharma.

Knowing your dharma activates your inner guidance system. It wakes up your living inner compass which guides you onto the path of high performance and high fulfillment. Without such an internal guidance system, it is easy to be tossed about by the fear-based thoughts and garbled messages arising from your habits of the past. Bringing this compass to life begins with discovering your core values.

Your Core Values

Your core values are the source of your passion and purpose. When you are connected to and acting from core values, you are energized, passionately engaged, and able to act with power and integrity. When you are disconnected from those core values your vitality evaporates, decision making is confused, and work frustrating.

Knowing your core values does not eliminate the inevitable challenges or changes of life, nor ensure a smooth ride. But it will provide you with one element of your living inner compass for staying on track during challenging times and for making wise choices that promote high performance and high fulfillment.

Inherited Values

Many people lose track of their core values growing up when they inherit values from a variety of sources. Some values come from families, others from schools and religious institutions. As you approach puberty, the influence of your families tends to wane, supplanted by that of your peers. Entering the world of work, you are further influenced by bosses and organizations. Behind it all is the constant drone of the media — radio, TV, movies, and advertising.

It is natural to adopt inherited values. As a child you look to adult authorities for guidance to provide you with principles for navigating the world. When you join an organization and enter a work culture, you look to your peers for guidance and advice on how to behave and succeed.

When your choices reflect inherited values, ideals, and opinions, however, your actions are governed by principles that come from others and not from your core. You may perform well, but if you are not aligned with your core values, passion and purpose are hard to sustain. When you use inherited values to guide your work life choices, you may drift off your own authentic leadership course.

> Only when you expose and examine your inherited values can you choose to accept, reject, or modify them.

The degree that you are unaware of your inherited values and beliefs is the degree to which they manage you. Only when you expose and examine your inherited values can you choose to accept, reject, or modify them.

Sayings You Hear Growing Up

Inherited values are passed on to you in many ways. One is in the form of sayings — those habitually repeated phrases that parents, teachers, bosses and other authorities chanted to you at the dinner table, in the classroom, from the pulpit, or at staff meetings. It is easy to accept those sayings and the values they contain without considering how they align with your core values.

One manager told me that one of the sayings she heard countless times while a child was, "You can't play until all the work is done." During a management retreat she reflected, "Through accepting this saying as a child I inherited values of hard work and responsibility. I am super-responsible. I stay late at the office and cannot leave until 'all the work is done.' What I am realizing is that all the work will never be done. And that I have been over responsible to the point of self sacrifice." Having spent two decades chained to her to-do list, this woman saw that her life was dangerously out of balance as a result of unconsciously living according to this inherited saying.

In another organization, a former CEO was known for saying, "You can say anything you want around here...on your last day." Although that CEO had been gone from the organization for seven years, the saying lived on amongst the company's employees, preserving a culture of fear, indirect communication, and low accountability.

Hidden Messages and Invisible Values

The sayings you inherited from family, bosses, and other authorities carry with them hidden values. As the sayings are repeated you absorb these values which can be like hitchhikers jumping onto a slow moving train. They enter your mind undetected, becoming part of the framework you unconsciously use to make decisions, take actions, and develop your career. These unexamined values shape how you understand the world and the ways in which you think and act.

In exploring her own inherited values one coaching client remembered her grandfather and the positive values of creativity, adventure, and learning that she inherited from him. She wrote:

My family heritage is Basque, an indigenous people who live in the Pyrenees mountains between Spain and France. The Basques call their newborns *walking stars* who have fallen to earth. This is how my maternal grandfather treated me — I was his *walking star.* He told me I could do anything I set my mind to. Grandpa delighted in my playfulness and creativity. We tap danced on the kitchen tiles. He sang to me in Spanish and Basque and told me stories of the old country. He encouraged my curiosity, studious nature, and independence. I inherited many wonderful values from him. He helped finance my two university degrees and supported my move to California...although we knew we'd miss each other terribly, and that he would most likely die when I was away.

Mixed Blessing

For many, inherited values are a mixed blessing that bring with them creative qualities and limiting qualities, aspects that nourish your growth and aspects that limit you. Karen, a participant in a leadership retreat, reported that she had received a mixed inheritance by internalizing the saying, "If it is worth doing, it is worth doing right."

Karen cherished her inherited values of passion and excellence. They kept her energized and engaged. But, she also inherited the limiting value of perfectionism. This limiting value caused Karen to be highly critical of herself and others. Collaboration was difficult and delegation a challenge. "A passionate atti-

> *You are heir to both the creative and limiting directives coded into your inherited values.*

tude of being fully committed to my work and to excellence is the creative part of my inheritance," she told the group. "The limiting part is that I am overly critical, a perfectionist, and uncomfortable with letting others get involved. What I'm learning is that my standards are not absolutes and, my need for control often blocks my own and others' creativity. Sometimes, an imperfect start is better than waiting for perfection before beginning."

Bob, the COO of Children's Hospital, inherited the saying, "If you can't say anything nice, don't say anything at all." The creative value that he identified with this saying was that of *compassion.* "I always consider others' feelings before I speak. I have a good sense of where others are at," Bob explained, "but the limiting value of this saying is *self-repression* or even *self-betrayal.* I will silence myself and not share my own views in order to keep the peace. I don't get my issues on the table and the group doesn't know what I really think."

Inherited values can be ambivalent. Even though the limiting values are unstated — you inherit them. You are heir to both the creative and limiting directives coded into your inherited values. As long as your inherited values go unexamined, you will remain caught in the unresolved tension between these creative and limiting aspects. The discord that is built into your inherited values lives within you as internal conflicts and misaligned intentions. When you are caught up in a vortex of inner discord — "Should I tell them what I think or keep silent?" — it is often an indicator that the two sides of your inherited values are struggling with each other.

High performance and high fulfillment is blocked by the contradictory structure of your inherited values. Your energy and attention is partially consumed by this tension. Resolving this structural tension liberates your energy and frees your creativity. Pushing away one side of your inherited values, even if it is the limiting side, simply aggravates the tension. It is like pushing on a spring to make it go away. As long as you keep applying pressure the spring will stay compressed but the moment your vigilance relaxes it springs back. Unless you can sustain your exertion of will power forever — and you can't — after a short time the original tension reasserts itself.

When uncovering your inherited values, it is useful to keep a neutral and curious attitude. Listen and discover, don't pre-judge. Notice what values you have inherited. Think about how they may be promoting or discouraging high performance and high fulfillment. By bringing awareness to the tensions of your inherited values their grip on your thinking relaxes. Tension dissolves when you hold it in the light of awareness.

Then you are free to discover the source of passion and purpose in your life — your core values.

Where Are They Leading?

What are the sayings about work that you heard while growing up? Did you hear "Nobody said work was supposed to be fun" or something more like, "Build your work around your passion"? Identifying your inherited values will reveal the hidden assumptions and beliefs that have been shaping your work.

Consider the implications of living according to inherited values. Where are they leading you? Is it a direction that you want for your work? If your inherited values ring true for you and if they are moving you in a direction you want — keep them. If not, recognize that it is time for an inner change.

If you sense that something is missing in your work, begin by asking yourself if your actions are being governed by inherited values. If so, and if the inherited values you identify don't belong to you, let them go.

Discovering Your Core Values

Claiming your core values can begin by recalling those people whom you admire and have positively influenced your life. The qualities that you admire in them are hints regarding your own core values. Who are your role models — those people that you look to for guidance? What is it about them that you respect so deeply?

You can also reflect on times of high performance

and high fulfillment in your life. What were the values that you were devoted to in those experiences? What values, even perhaps without knowing it at the time, were you living? What was the passion that animated and motivated you?

The process of claiming core values is one of stripping away layers of inherited values and more superficial motivations to touch the heart of your deepest driving force. Discovering your core values reveals something that you have always known — but may have forgotten — that at your core you are passionate and purposeful.

Reflection & Dialogue: Core Values

Personal Reflection

Set aside at least 30 minutes to reflect on and identify your core values.

Stage 1: Identify Inherited Values

Write down the values and beliefs about work, success, leadership, and your abilities that you inherited from parents, teachers, bosses, and other key authorities.

What are the sayings about work you inherited from parents, mentors, and others? Identify the creative and limiting values that came with each saying.

Example saying: If you want it done right, do it yourself.

Inherited creative values: autonomy, responsibility

Inherited limiting values: control, over-responsibility

Step 2: Set Inherited Values Aside

Symbolically set these inherited values aside and mentally affirm: I am no longer guiding my work life using these values and beliefs.

Step 3: Sort Core Values — Yes and No

Review the list of core values on page 65 and check off those that are linked to your passion and purpose. Cross out those that are not.

Remember, the key to this process is being open and honest with yourself. This is an exercise in reconnecting to the source of passion and purpose within. Tell yourself the truth about those values that feed your soul.

Step 4: Sorting for Top Ten Core Values

Look at those values you have said "yes" to. Sort through them for those that are most primary and core for you. This requires both a willingness to let go of certain values and a willingness to honestly choose those that are yours. Pick your top ten.

As you complete this stage of your discovery process, consider that a value is a core value if:

• You choose it freely

• You prize and cherish it

• You're willing to publicly affirm it

• You act upon it regularly

Step 5: Hone in on Your Three Core Values

Take your top ten and select those values that are the three most core. Remember that you are not denigrating the other many excellent values. You are simply choosing those that are most primary, central, core to your energy, passion, and purpose.

Step 6: Define Your Unique Meaning

Write down your individual meaning for each of your three core values. What does it mean to you to live this value fully and authentically?

Learning Partner Dialogue

Share your core values with each other. Listen to each person's unique meaning. Discuss how to support each person in living their core values. Ask for feedback on how you are living your values. Ask for feedback on where you could be more congruent with your core values.

CORE VALUES

___ Achievement

___ Adventure

___ Awareness

___ Balance

___ Beauty

___ Challenge

___ Change

___ Commitment

___ Community

___ Compassion

___ Creativity

___ Excellence

___ Flexibility

___ Freedom

___ Growth

___ Happiness

___ Influence

___ Integrity

___ Intimacy

___ Joy

___ Leadership

___ Learning

___ Love

___ Loyalty

___ Making a Difference

___ Mastery

___ Nature

___ Order

___ Peace

___ Play

___ Privacy

___ Prosperity

___ Reflection

___ Security

___ Service

___ Spirituality

___ Success

___ Taking Care of Loved Ones

___ Trust

___ Truth

___ Well Being

___ Wholeness

___ Wisdom

What was it like to identify your core values? Many people tell me that this is a hard process. They find themselves wrestling with which values to keep and which to discard. They often have to work their way through layers of inherited beliefs and sometimes feel guilty eliminating a value that they have been taught to esteem.

Walking Your Talk

Discovering and claiming your core values is one thing. Living these values is another. In order to walk your talk and align your actions with your values it is essential that you define what it looks like — for you — to live each of your core values.

No dictionary can define your values for you. You must articulate yourself what it means to live your values. You will need to break free from the pull of inherited definitions and seek to honestly and courageously think for yourself. In developing your unique meaning for each of your values you start to shape your own definition of high performance and high fulfillment. Although you draw from your past experiences, your unique meaning filters out the inherited contradictions and clearly states what it means for you to live authentically.

For example, one of my core values is wisdom. My definition of wisdom is: To be a student of life; to seek the universal principles that govern life and to align with them; to be open and actively learning; and to listen deeply to people and situations before acting.

Another value of mine is service. My definition of service is: To act in ways that support others to discover and act on their deepest truth. These definitions allow me to reflect on the degree to which my daily actions express my values.

When my son Nathaniel announced that he was dropping out of college, I didn't take it too well. I was not open. I did not listen deeply. I wasn't really focused on his deepest truth. In fact, I didn't let him get out another word before I launched into an impassioned lecture on the importance of education and the quest for knowledge. If there had been a soapbox to stand on, I would have stepped right up.

"Do you want to learn about what I'm thinking?" Nathaniel asked when I took a breath.

His question stopped me. Was I interested in learning about my son's thoughts and experiences? Was I open to listening or did I want to continue my lecture? To be honest, I was torn. And in being torn, I was barely aligned with my own values. It took several deep breaths before I could begin to listen and to learn about my son's plans to accept a one-year

It becomes your leadership responsibility to live with more awareness and integrity.

position coordinating the national youth leadership programs for his church.

As you reconnect to your core values, and reflect on your behaviors, you may find it necessary to make changes that align how you act with your own values. Sometimes it is hard to see the ways in which you don't walk your own talk or embody your own values. It is easier to see the ways in which others are out of alignment with what matters most to you.

If truth is among your core values, it will be important for you to experience truthfulness in your workplace. If you are experiencing a lack of truthfulness, ask yourself what aspects of your work experience are misaligned with that core value. Although you may see clearly that others are not living up to your standard of truthfulness, you may not see how you are withholding or not expressing your core value of truthfulness.

It's Not Them, It's You

The shortfall of others, and lack of truthfulness in the culture can be so clear it seems hard to believe that the change must begin with you. Yet, I believe it is true. This is where your learning partners can be helpful. Their detached perspective and thoughtful listening can help you step back and see the ways in which your reactivity may be compromising your own values and diminishing your ability to transform the situation.

Following an organizational restructuring, George was promoted to director of the communications department. The former director was reassigned to an international business department. The transition meeting was cordial, but in the weeks that followed George became aware that the former director was covertly "managing and monitoring" several of her old projects behind his back. When George asked about this, she tried to smooth things over and minimize the issue by insisting, "I just want to keep in touch with old friends and co-workers. You can't really object to that. I've been their contact person for seven years."

George ended the conversation politely but inside he was frustrated and angry. "She is undermining my authority. She is being dishonest. I don't trust her to tell me the truth." With coaching and reflection, George saw that while the former manager was indeed being untruthful, so was he. His politeness was a smoke screen that kept him from being direct about his concerns. His frustration and anger was also with himself as he had betrayed his own value of truthfulness and was now complaining behind her back. In short, he was not being a model of truthfulness.

"I can easily see her being untruthful. It is hard to admit my part," he told me. "But, I see that I have been prolonging the problem by not being truthful and instead trying to indirectly manipulate the situation."

Because inherited values and emotional reactions are often operating invisibly, one may be espousing one thing — truthfulness — yet enacting a contradictory set of behaviors. You can see these incongruities in others. You typically do not see the ways your walk doesn't match your talk. "You must be the change you want to see in the world," said the great Indian leader Mahatma Gandhi.

At an annual leadership retreat for senior executives in the Federal Government, participants work on defining their core values. One of the questions I always ask is, "What would it look like for you to fully express your values in your work and workplace?"

Last year a man came up to me during the midmorning break. He told me that he had struggled with "even thinking that I could express my value of spirituality at work." This cherished value was one that he had assumed could only find expression in his activities at church and in his volunteer work. But in talking with a colleague during the exercise, he began to see a different choice. His colleague told him, "For me, spirituality at work means being fully attentive to every person I talk with. It means seeing that people are more than 'human resources' they are human beings. I care about their work and I care about them as individuals. That is one of the ways I live my spirituality at work."

> *The mirroring nature of experience becomes life's way of teaching and coaching you.*

When you perceive one of your core values to be lacking in a situation or relationship, check first on how fully you are expressing that value. Accept your experience of their lack as a mirror reflecting your own inner imbalance. The mirroring nature of your experience then becomes life's way of teaching and coaching you to grow in awareness and more fully embody your core values.

If you are surrounded by supportive like-minded people, it takes little courage to live your values. But the world is complicated. Facing the challenges around you reveals the complications within you. You are challenged to take a deeper dive into your core values and embody them more fully. This takes courage, particularly when those around you seem to be the problem and you feel unsafe in that environment. This is when the courage to whole-heartedly live your values is most needed. As my friend Bob Anderson of The Leadership Circle puts it, "There is no safe place to be courageous."

Living congruent with your values is among the most powerful leadership tools available. Substantive change in the world around you may hinge on whether or not you are willing to do most of the changing. Taking this proposition deeply to heart, without any sense of heroics, brings the importance of core values into focus. Your own congruence is part of the congruence of the world around you. As you live your values more fully, those values are more present wherever you are.

Following Inner Guidance

The ultimate goal of defining and reflecting on your core values is to become the living expression of those qualities in daily life. Your values are more than ideas — they are the wellspring of your passion and purpose. As your connection to your core values deepens you will learn what it feels like to live them. You will develop the inner guidance system that alerts you when you are in or out of alignment with your values. You will learn to use and trust your inner guidance and enjoy the dynamic interplay of inner guidance and outer events as you learn to make shifts in attitude and actions that deepen your connection to core values.

Remember the childhood game of "telephone" where a message is progressively whispered from person to person and finally spoken aloud? The predictable and hilarious result was a garbled version of the original message reshaped by the interpretations, assumptions, and deletions of many receivers. You can be in a similar situation when you first attune to the feeling guidance of your core values.

The more you feel the connection to your core values the more you can turn to them for guidance and insight. When you are congruent with your core values there is positive, vibrant, joyful feeling in your body. When you are out of alignment with your core values tensions, tightness, and other unpleasant feelings arise. You may begin to re-experience the familiar conflict between the two sides of your inherited values. But, now your inner guidance alerts you and keeps you out of the fracas. Instead of being drawn into an all too familiar fight, you shift and align with the positive feelings of your core values. A deep connection with your values frees you from the cacophony of monkey mind voices in order to discern the authentic presence of your passion and purpose guiding you from deep within. This completes the first step of awakening your inner guidance system. You have discerned the difference between inherited values and core values; discovered your three core values; defined your unique meanings; and learned about the importance of using them for inner guidance as you move yourself towards greater levels of high performance and high fulfillment.

Reflection & Dialogue: Integrating Core Values

Personal Reflection

For the next three days, set aside 10 minutes of quiet time in the morning before you go to work for yourself.

• Reflect on your core values and how you can express these positive qualities in your workday. Think about how you would like to express those values in the meetings, conversations, and events of the day. Make a clear mental picture of what it will look like for you to live your values.

At the end of the day, take another 10 minutes of quiet time for reflecting on what happened.

• Reflect on those incidents where you acted in alignment with your core values. Don't look for the grand gesture. Rather, recall examples of ordinary behaviors and interactions that reflect your core values. Note also incidents where you struggled to live your values, where you abandoned them to some degree, and mentally note how you might have expressed them more fully.

For all examples consider:

Where did the examples occur?

Whom were you with?

What did you do?

How did you feel?

What does this suggest to you about living your values?

It is by setting a daily intention and then reflecting on your performance that your core values will come alive for you at work.

Learning Partner Dialogue

Share with your learning partners examples of where you expressed your values and where you were out of congruence. Explore the thoughts, beliefs, emotions that shifted you out of alignment with core values.

Discuss what these experiences suggest about living your core values.

Ask for feedback on where you are living your values.

Ask for feedback on where you could be more congruent with your core values.

5

YOUR UNIQUE GIFTS

Maturity is a time when we stop hiding our
strengths from ourselves out of fear and begin to
live at our best level — instead of below it.

Dag Hammarskjold

The second element of your inner guidance system is your gifts. I define gifts as your unique expression of greatness. To enjoy a life of high performance and high fulfillment, you must identify, develop, and use your unique gifts. When you are expressing your gifts you maximize your experience of high performance; you are better at what you do. When you use your gifts you experience high fulfillment; it is energizing and joyful.

Your gifts are inherent to who you are. They are woven into the fabric of your being. To neglect your gifts is to neglect what you were designed to do in this life. When you spend your time in activities that do not tap your gifts, you reduce your ability to fully contribute to the world. "There is a vitality, a life force, an energy, a quickening that is translated through you into action. And because there is only one of you in all time, this expression is unique. If you block it, it will never exist through any other medium and will be lost. The world will not have it," said Martha Graham, the visionary modern dancer and choreographer.

You are a unique expression of life's presence. You are a uniquely designed instrument. Using your gifts develops your expertise in tuning and playing the instrument you have been given. When you give your gifts, you tap that vitality that Graham refers to, and give expression to the power that life has entrusted to you.

More than Personal

The greatness that Graham points towards is beyond the personal. She compares it to a universal energy that is modulated into a unique frequency as it flows through your specific behaviors and ways of being.

Sometimes it is hard to admit your own greatness. You may have been trained to regard yourself as "no better than anybody else." You may have inherited the limiting belief that greatness is for the few. But in fact, you already have a unique style and presence in the world — your gifts are your unique expression of greatness.

It may seem that I am exaggerating by attributing such immensity to your ordinary abilities. However, consider that scientists tell us that the universe began as a big bang, and your body, brain, nervous system, the instruments through which you express your gifts are the outcome of that original big bang. On a purely physical level, you are made of cosmic material.

From a genetic perspective, you are the product of thousands of years of cellular mixing and matching.

Your current abilities are the expression of mind-boggling genetic mathematics — the way you walk, talk, think and act is woven from the DNA strands of your ancestors. Your talents are their gift to you encoded into your cells.

From a spiritual perspective you are a soul with a unique purpose to fulfill. Through fulfilling that purpose you bring healing and wholeness to yourself and the world. This is why you are here in this life. You fulfill your purpose by remembering, developing, and offering your gifts to the world.

Everything you are and everything you have has been gifted to you — whether from the cosmic dust, your ancestors, a higher source, or all three. These are simply different ways of trying to *Universal energy is modulated into a unique frequency as it flows through your specific behaviors and ways of being.* put into words the immensity of what has been given to you. However you describe it — the mystery remains — life's gifts are present in you.

As you appreciate your gifts, the natural impulse is to consciously seek ways to express them in your daily actions. Your work begins to become more enjoyable and your contribution more complete. The more you understand what creates high performance and high fulfillment, the more you are naturally drawn to use your gifts in service. The authentic response to being gifted is to give. You realize that you renew and enhance your gifts by giving what you have been given. Through your service the circle is complete. Life gives and receives endlessly through you and to you. When you consciously enter into this gifting cycle, you enhance your ability to perform and your experience of fulfillment.

Unwrapping the Gift

It is easy to recognize the presence of gifts in people who excel in their field. But how do you discern your own gifts? Consider the gift of compassionate caring. Who embodies compassion through their actions in the world? Perhaps you think of Mother Teresa, the Dalai Lama, or Albert Schweitzer. Who embodies the gift of creativity? Well-known examples include Pablo Picasso or Walt Disney. What about the gift of humor? Mark Twain, Robin Williams, or Chris Rock might come to mind. For the gifts of compassion, creativity, and humor you can certainly name lesser-known people who fully and uniquely embody and express these talents through their daily actions. High performance and high fulfillment comes from fully and consciously employing one's gifts. Jim, CEO of a mental health facility, is a gifted listener. When you talk with him, you feel that everything else in his busy world has dropped out of mind. He focuses and absorbs not just the words that are spoken but the unspoken meanings behind them.

Christine, the director of laboratory services for a large health care system, is gifted at seeing the big picture and communicating complex ideas in easy-to-understand ways. She is gifted at motivating her staff to see how their individual work contributes to a larger purpose.

Joan, an engineer, is gifted at tapping people's

innate motivations and talents. She has a track record of turning around failing projects and reviving the spirit of demoralized teams. She inspires people with her positive energy and good-humored persistence.

Through the use of your gifts, you can lift the execution of simple tasks to the level of artistry. My grandparents designed and sold women's hats. Their business, H. Starr Millinery, prospered throughout the 1930s and '40s in New York City when fashionable hats were the rage. My grandmother was a gifted designer who could twist and fold a length of red ribbon into a silken rose. She relished the process of combining beads, feathers, and ribbons in unique and beautiful combinations. For her, each hat was a work of art. Along with her artistic gifts, my grandmother was incredibly gregarious. She loved people and enjoyed learning about each person's unique history. In the family it was said that she had "the gift of gab."

My grandmother's gifts for design, relationship building, and communication found ample expression in her work. She traveled throughout Europe, building enduring relationships with craftspeople and manufacturers in her search for unique millinery materials. She used her communication skills in sales, making the buying process into an enjoyable experience of theater for her customers.

Clues From Your Past

When you reflect on times in your work life that are fully engaging, meaningful, and purposeful, you will find clues to your gifts — your unique expression of greatness. Consider examples from different times in your life — what were the talents that made the experience alive for you? What are the activities that absorb you now to the point that you lose track of time happily immersed in the task? Do you love working with numbers, mediating interpersonal disputes, teaching, planning, or building things? See yourself actually doing these activities, and consider the following questions:

- What patterns of action consistently appear in your high performance-high fulfillment experiences?
- What activities are most energizing and engaging?
- What kinds of challenges tap your gifts?

Your gifts are those actions that:

Generate energy

You feel more alive, more vital when you are exercising your unique talents and you feel the energy of life coursing through us. There is a sense of enthusiasm even when situations are tough. In fact, challenges often hone and deepen the gifts. In contrast, non-gift activities are energy drainers. They sap vitality and require constant monitoring and effort to sustain.

Intrinsically rewarding

Exercising and expressing your gifts is rewarding in and of itself. There is an inherent fulfillment that comes from developing your gifts. When you use your gifts in your work, and get paid for it, it is like an extra bonus — the icing on the cake. Using your gifts connects you to your primary motivation, you love to be engaged in these activities.

Fundamental to who you are

Like Mother Teresa's gift of compassion or Robin Williams' gift of humor, your gifts are fundamental to who you are. If you have a gift for teaching you will find "teachable" moments everywhere in your life. If you have a gift for leading you will find yourself in leadership roles in many places in your life. Sometimes your gifts are so much a part of you that you cannot see them. They are so fundamental to who you are and how you do things that you take them for granted. Others can provide invaluable feedback — friends, family members, and colleagues can help you define your gifts. In the end, however, you need to claim your greatness.

Timeless

When you use your gifts it is easy to lose track of time. You move into what athletes call "the zone" and mystics call "the eternal now." All of your attention is rapt and committed to the task at hand. This quality of intense focus is natural, not forced. Forced attention makes time drag on and on (remember sitting in a class you didn't like and watching the clock move with such painful slowness that minutes felt like hours). The natural absorption of attention dissolves your familiar sense of time into a joyful experience of timelessness.

Serve others

Your gifts are not for yourself alone, they are for the benefit of others. Your gifts are for life. When you are using your gifts, you are maximizing high performance by bringing your best self, your best abilities to the table. The double win of using your gifts is that along with high performance you experience high fulfillment.

It's Elementary

An ancient intuition regarding the structure of the soul can help you identify your gifts. The ancient wisdom traditions suggest that underneath individual differences and the endless variations of human behavior are common themes, patterns of reaction, ways of perceiving, and modes of action. The ancients simplified the complexity of the soul into a few primal energies. These primal energies combine and recombine to give rise to infinite patterns of expression. Your individual giftedness is a unique expression of those basic energies.

From India, to Greece, to Europe, to the Native American traditions, from the most ancient past to more recent times, philosophers, visionaries, and social scientists have identified four primary or elemental types that comprise the inner structure of the person. While the labels, language, and symbolism may vary with the times or with a particular culture, this ancient and pervasive insight points to an important underlying structure. This four-fold structure appears to be almost universally acknowledged.

Four-Fold Structure

This four-fold structure has consistently been linked to four universal elements: fire, earth, air, and water. These are the primal energies that give rise to your individual gifts. The challenge for modern minds is to understand that these universal elements are not the chemical elements listed on the periodic table. The elements of fire, earth, air, and water are best understood as universal functions which describe a set of energies or gifts. These energies can be observed in individuals and in the natural world. The same energetic expressions — of fiery intensity, earthy steadiness, airy openness, and watery depths — are found in both human behavior and in nature. You are, after all, part of nature.

These ancient intuitions regarding the elements are preserved in our everyday language. We describe people as being down-to-earth or stuck in the mud; as being fired with enthusiasm or too hot to handle; as being a breath of fresh air or having their head in the clouds; of having great depths or of being all wet.

In modern times, the pioneering psychologist Carl Jung linked the four universal elements to four functions of the psyche. He related fire to intuition, water to feeling, air to thinking, and earth to sensation. Echoing the ancient understanding, Jung suggested that while you contain all the elements, you have a natural affinity for and develop one or two more than the others.

Four Elements

The following descriptions of the elements are meant to provide you with language and insights to better understand your gifts and strengthen your ability to use your gifts creatively. These descriptions are not meant to limit or pigeonhole you. Although, you are infinitely more complex than any description or list can indicate, there is a design or structure to your soul. You are gifted in particular ways and embody a unique set of gifts. When the patterns of your soul become rigid, they imprison you. When you use them consciously to enrich your life and your world, they promote high performance and high fulfillment. Use this model to learn, not label. Do not confuse the map for the territory it describes. Use the map to journey more deeply into your expression of authentic leadership.

Gift of Fire

When the element of fire is active in your being you have visionary gifts. You will tend to look to the future and be impatient with those who look backward for insight or meaning. The fiery element sparks the spirit of adventure, impulsiveness, and enthusiasm. Those with much fire in their being love new experiences and are drawn to action and spontaneity. They prefer learning "hands-on" and like to see immediate results. Fire gives the ability to make quick decisions, as this element gives one the gift of visualizing the end result without much analysis. This engenders an action-oriented approach to life. People with a lot of fire can work well in groups as long as things move along and they are the center of attention. Fire thrives on unpredictability, which works well in an atmosphere of change. Fire energy can feel confined by structures that require details and deliberation. It is bored easily, and always seeks ways to rekindle the flame of enthusiasm.

Fire energy is...	Fire Gifts include...
Ambitious	Setting and achieving goals
Visionary	Envisioning the future
Courageous	Taking charge
Confident	Rallying others to the cause
Independent	Competing to win
Determined	Inspiring others
In Control	Setting the pace
Goal Oriented	Being decisive

Gift of Water

When the element of water is active in your being, you will be gifted with emotional intelligence. The water element is fluid and adaptable with a focus on building and strengthening relationships. This energy gives the ability to instinctively nurture and empathize. Water can bring depth and the capacity for inner reflection. When this element is strong, people base their decisions on past experiences, feelings, and intuition. Water strengthens one's capacity to feel shifts in the emotional well-being of others and to understand people at a deep inner level. Because of its depth and sensitivity, water is attuned to the unspoken needs and dreams hidden within individuals and groups. With gentleness and skill, water brings life to that which is deeply buried within. Water energy is gifted at teaching and mentoring, experiencing profound gratification from helping others develop.

Water energy is...	Water gifts include...
Understanding	Mediating conflict
Intuitive	Teaching
Easy going	Working on teams
Supportive	Using diplomacy
Compassionate	Encouraging, understanding others
Genuine	Facilitating groups
Reflective	Selling
Nurturing	Putting people at ease

Gift of Earth

When the element of Earth is active in your being, you will have practical gifts. You concentrate on what works. The Earth element energizes the no-nonsense spirit of persistence and the drive towards implementation. Earth energy is oriented to the present. It is realistic, traditional, and rule-oriented. Earth is willing to take on big projects, shoulder the burden and pursue what matters with patience and self-discipline. This element is gifted at organizing and planning in any area of life. Earth energy is timely, sensible, establishes a stable foundation that others can build on. The earth quality is grounded and gives the ability to maintain structure, set and keep boundaries, and uphold tradition.

Earth energy is...	Earth gifts include...
Focused	Detailed planning
Industrious	Trouble-shooting
Loyal	Organizing anything
Practical	Doing it right the first time
Well-prepared	Creating systems
Dependable	Keeping teams on track
Logical, analytical	Accepting responsibility

Gift of Air

When the element of Air is active in your being, you will have intellectual and communication gifts. Your mind is active and able to step back and look at situations from a broad, detached perspective. It thrives on ideas and interaction. This energy is gifted at collecting data, connecting ideas, and pulling diverse concepts together in an integrated model or body of knowledge. Air energy is everywhere touching everything and thus gives the ability to see how ideas and principles are interconnected. Air increases curiosity, adaptability, and the desire to learn and understand. Air thrives on puzzles and problems applying the gift of rationality to discovering solutions. When air is active decisions are based on data and information, not intuition. Air lives in the realm of the mind and is gifted at written and verbal communication.

Air energy is...	Air gifts include...
Spontaneous	Adapting to change
Curious	Expanding limits
Communicative	Improvising
Multi-tasking	Writing
Analytical	Speaking
Innovative	Explaining
Idea-centered	Motivating others through ideas
Flexible	Starting new projects

Primary Element

While you include all of the elements, they are not equally strong. Some of your soul's muscle groups are stronger than others. Your primary element is the one that is most natural to you. It is your greatest strength and contains your core gifts. You have ready access to the gifts of that element. You use those gifts effortlessly and you are able to consciously refine your expression of those gifts most easily.

The element that is next most developed is called your supporting element. It augments your primary gifts and expands your ways of being and acting. When you are able to channel these soul strengths into specific skills and then use those skills in your work, you maximize high performance and high fulfillment.

Getting Feedback

One of the most effective things you can do to increase your awareness and develop your gifts is to request feedback. Invest yourself in learning from others. This chapter has introduced to you an ancient way of identifying your gifts. Be curious to learn how your assessment matches with what others who know you may think. Be open to listening to them. Ask for examples. Get their ideas on how you can grow and develop your gifts.

Ask five different people who know you in different contexts about your gifts. Although this can be embarrassing, try to work through it. Remember, claiming your gifts is not a competition. It has nothing to do with being better (or worse) than others. It is about your unique greatness and along with core values is part of your inner leadership compass.

Navigating work and life with high performance and high fulfillment means living your values and using your gifts. Think of your current work, and consider which of your gifts are being fully utilized, partially utilized, and which are currently untapped.

MY GIFTS THAT ARE:		
FULLY UTILIZED	PARTIALLY UTILIZED	UNTAPPED

"The most exhausting thing in my life is being insincere," wrote author Anne Morrow Lindbergh. To be yourself — the authentic leader that you were designed to be — involves using and developing your gifts in your current work.

Determine how you can begin to express more of your gifts at work. Who do you need to approach about your ideas? How can you start in small ways? What kinds of conversations or actions do you need to take to create work that taps your natural gifts?

Reflection & Dialogue: Your Gifts

Personal Reflection

What are your primary and supporting elements?

How do you express these at work?

Which elements do you work most easily with?

Which do you find more challenging?

Learning Partner Dialogue

Share your primary and supportive elements.

Give each other feedback on how these elements are positively expressed at work.

Discuss the connection between your elements and your values.

What are the benefits and challenges of having all elements represented on a team or department?

6

YOUR CALLING

Whom or what are you choosing to serve right now? It takes courage to ask this question of yourself. But without courage, you can't practice any other value consistently.

Maya Angelou

Along with identifying core values and claiming elemental gifts, the final factor that makes up the inner compass is your calling. Your calling is the central imperative of your soul. It is what you most want to experience and express in your life.

When you were a child, you may have had intimations and hints regarding your calling. Relatives and strangers asked "What do you want to be when you grow up?" As a child your answers to the question — a cowboy, a doctor, a movie star, a dancer — were often more symbolic than predictive of future career choices. You answered from your own limited knowledge of what was possible in the world. The role you find yourself in now is typically quite different from those you imagined as a young person. Although, often your early intuitions told a deeper truth about your core purpose than a job title can reveal. My friend Jim Stuart told me,

As a child, I wanted to be a minister to comfort others and live in God's embrace. In my twenties

I leapt into the adventure of life as a student and then a Naval Officer. In my thirties, I joined the company founded by my grandfather where my father was CEO. For decades I struggled to find my place and passion in the boardroom. Then through a series of dramatic reversals in my personal and business life, I left the corporate world. I began to question, study, and reconnect with my real deeper purpose. Now in my 60s, I know my childhood instincts were right. I am a minister in an un-ordained and non-traditional mold. My purpose is to help people to belong, live purposefully, to discover the power of wholeness. Integration. Wholeness. Holiness. The same word root and the root impulse of my childhood.

Your calling is what gives meaning to your life, and direction to the roles you fulfill. The environment in which you work typically defines your job description. But the purpose that gives life to the official description comes from you.

You don't need to invent this calling. You need to discern it and open up to it. When you open, your calling finds you and carries you forward, deeper into what it means for you to exercise authentic leadership. A door opens right in the middle of your everyday experience through which you can express your core values and offer your innate gifts. Opening to your calling builds the bridge between your inner being and the world.

Knowing your calling completes the inner guidance system, that living compass by which you navigate the conditions of your work life with clarity, confidence, and congruence.

Seeing the Hidden Image

Several years ago, when walking through any major metropolitan airport, you would find small groups of travelers standing and staring at what appeared to be large abstract designs. These were complex graphics called Magic Eye or stereogram images in which a three dimensional image is hidden within a two dimensional pattern. The three dimensional image is hidden in plain sight. It simply requires a special way

Opening to your calling builds the bridge between your inner being and the world.

of "focusing" in order for that which is concealed to emerge into view. It is the same with your calling. It is there and it emerges as you learn to focus and discern its presence.

As you align with your calling the sense of rightness is tangible, not conceptual. Things can be going poorly, full of delays and obstacles. But through it all you feel a palpable quality of aliveness that sharpens your awareness and deepens your appreciation of the present moment. You know that what you are doing matters and that your actions, even the smallest gesture, contribute to something valuable. You experience your connection with others and with something larger than yourself.

And you perceive that larger purpose to which your actions contribute.

A commitment to realizing your calling makes each moment precious, because each moment, each conversation, decision, and interaction, is an opportunity to align with your calling. Opening to the impulse of your calling brings your values to life and provides a channel through which the energy of your gifts can flow. When your attention and actions are in line with your calling, you experience high performance and high fulfillment.

Calling Is Not a Goal

Your calling is different from your goals. Goals are highly defined, specific, time-bound results. A goal can be completed. When you cross the finish line, you've arrived. When the project is over, it is time for the next assignment. But your calling is not something you finish. There is no final finish line to cross. Your calling is always unfolding in a spiral of expanded clarity and creativity.

If developing the capacity for high performance and high fulfillment is a journey, then goals are destinations, stopping points along way. Your calling is the direction in which you are traveling, not any particular goal. It is the way you follow to discover and deepen your expression of authentic leadership, not the end results you create. Living and working with purpose keeps you heading in the direction of your calling.

Fidelity to your calling helps you select goals that matter. Knowing your calling clarifies what is worth doing and what is superfluous. Goals that follow the arc of your essential direction are worthy of attention. Until you discern the path of your calling and are heading towards your true North many side roads can seem inviting.

Calling Is Not Ambition

Ambition is pursuing achievements because attaining them will be impressive. Ambition seeks to attract the attention and admiration of others. Ambition is the shadow side of calling. When pursuing ambition you are driven to look good on paper, to make it, to gain prestige or fame. These are substitute states of

Each moment, each conversation, decision, and interaction, is an opportunity to align with your calling.

fulfillment that pale beside the bone-deep contentment that comes from following one's calling. Following your calling does not always dictate a change in the role you perform, but it often requires that you transform the way you inhabit that role.

Prematurely changing roles before having discerned your calling can be a way of avoiding the deeper inquiry that authentic leadership requires. You can make changes in your work life motivated by ambition or avoidance instead of by the soulful desire to contribute, create, and live more whole heartedly.

The deep work of pursuing your calling demands change that is more than cosmetic. You do not suddenly embody your values, claim your gifts, or follow your essential purpose by changing roles, leaving the organization, and moving on. It is often easier to make external changes than to take the time to discern whether your dissatisfaction is with the job or with your own misalignment with your purpose.

Be Willing to Tear Up the Bathroom

When my wife suggested that we remodel our bathroom it did not seem like a big project. Deborah and I wanted to turn a pink fifties-style bathroom into a beautiful spa-retreat. We wanted a place to take a steam, relax in the jacuzzi, unwind and rejuvenate; a place of simplicity, stone, and warm, earthy colors.

The first stage in the process was demolition. It took four guys to carry out the old cast iron tub. I was eager to have a restful, earthy retreat. But what was left, after the contractor disappeared, was just earth. The tub was gone, the floor too. What was left was just dirt, earth, *terra firma.*

We had imagined simplicity. What we had was more than simple. It was primitive. Crossing the threshold from the hallway into the bathroom was like stepping back in time, into an era before electricity and indoor plumbing — to a time of dirt houses and earthen floors.

Without the walls or floors the original sixty-year-old joists were visible. Some were charred, apparently from fire damage, and some were rotting. "This is good," my wife would tell me, "we need to see what is there." Deborah understands the value of exposing the crumbling structures that are hidden beneath the surface of things. "This is what happens when you remodel an old house," she told me. "You find things that were hidden and need to be cared for."

If you want to serve with passion, create with meaning, and lead with authenticity, you may need to do some inner remodeling work. Finding your way back to your calling can require some digging and some discernment. You do not reach high performance and high fulfillment by surface readjustments or quick fixes. If you choose to serve with passion, create with meaning, and lead with authenticity, you have to work from within outwards.

Double Doors to Calling

You discern the shape of your calling in two ways. One is by learning to purify your hopes. The other is by learning to respect and attend to your fears or wounds. Your hopes call you forward into life. They stretch you to expand your vision of who you are and what you can offer to enrich your world. Your fears stretch you as well. They call you inward and downward into the depths of the soul where you can contact and take care of your vulnerabilities and longings.

Your calling is linked to both. These two, your hopes and your fears, are like double doors leading to knowledge of your calling. You have to grasp the handles on both doors in order to pass through.

It can seem as though your hopes and your fears are in conflict with each other. Focusing on hopes, aspirations, and dreams is more appealing than dwelling in the sensitive and often overwhelming place of fear. But knowledge of your authentic calling comes through facing this polarity — your dreams and doubts, your hopes and fears — truthfully. Hopes seem to lift you up. Fears seem to drag you down.

But when you take the time to honestly examine your hopes, you find mixed motivations. To a certain degree your hopes are real expressions of what matters most to you. And to a certain degree they are strategies for proving yourself worthy in some way.

You see that you do want to live your values but you also want some applause along the way. You want safe passage to the island of success. The mixed motivations that permeate your hopes can limit your capacity for high performance and high fulfillment. Your fears can paralyze your forward movement. Facing these mixed motivations and confronting your fears without flinching, turning away, or rationalizing, generates an inner heat that is clarifying. The strength to accept and live your calling is forged in that heat.

7

CHAINSAW ARMADILLOS

If you bring forth what is within you,
what you bring forth will save you.
If you do not bring forth what is within you,
what you do not bring forth will destroy you.

Gospel of Thomas

When you take time to honestly examine your fears, you find something unexpected. You find a tenderness that is linked to your soul's longing for wholeness and service. This tenderness protects the lost parts of yourself. You need these missing parts in order to fulfill your calling.

Courageously moving towards your fears and experiencing your tender heart generates inner fire. Going into this tenderness you feel the heat. Your authenticity is forged in that heat. Honestly examining your hopes and purifying them of self-serving ambition also generates inner fire. What cannot be avoided is the fire.

Hopes and Fears

When talking about hopes, fears, and facing this fire with my colleague, Jim Lemmer, he told me how he had glimpsed the relationship between hopes and fears while on a road trip to the Southwest.

Jim was driving through a long stretch of anonymous highway in Northern Arizona enjoying the views of abandoned buildings and cars disintegrating in the hot dry air. Every so often he passed through a small town, each one much like the last

Chainsaw armadillos are your unacknow-ledged fears that spring to life when the most vulnerable parts of you are touched.

— filling station, general store, a bar or maybe an auto parts outfit. It was at the center of one of these towns that Jim suddenly understood the relationship between hope and fear.

He had slowed down for the town's lone stop sign when he heard the cough of a two-stroke motor starting up. Jim looked to his left and there was a rangy, middle-aged man with a two-day growth on his chin, wearing dirt-colored work boots, old Levi 501s, and a faded green t-shirt. Jim knew immediately who he was because of the sign next to the guy's lawn chair that read "CHAINSAW ARMADILLOS : $10–$20." The other clue was the little army of carved armadillos huddled around him.

"That's when it hit me," Jim said.

"What?" I asked.

"The reason people hold back from their calling."

"Because of chainsaw armadillos?"

"Absolutely. Everyone thinks they're going to end up like the Chainsaw Armadillo guy. Deep down in the recesses of your brain there's this little fear button. When it gets pushed, you start thinking about chainsaw armadillos.

Here's how it happens: You are driving home from work or sitting in a meeting or doing something else that you've done a thousand times. You are barely paying attention when something happens to you. You have an insight, a sizzling realization. It sparkles in your head and sends shivers up your spine. You know what you need to do in order to transform your work. You know what you have to say and who you need to talk with." Jim paused for breath.

"Then in the blink of an eye — that fear button buried deep in your brain treats you to a full color movie of what will happen if you speak or act authentically. You see yourself on the big screen and remember this all happens in a nano-second being laughed out of the room, losing your job, your house, your reputation, the respect of your kids and your peers, as well as all your savings. Jump-cut to a blue lawn chair somewhere in a vast expanse of featureless badlands. There you are, carving chainsaw armadillos at 10 bucks a pop."

Most people have seen some version of the Chain-saw Armadillo movie with evocative images so potent that they avoid the path of purpose and squash their authenticity. Chainsaw armadillos are your unacknow-ledged fears. They spring to life when the most vulnerable parts of you are touched.

Reflection & Dialogue: Healing Wounds

Personal Reflection

What are the chainsaw armadillos (the fearful thoughts) that keep you from fully pursuing high performance and high fulfillment?

What is a persistent hope or aspiration of yours? What about this connects to your core values and feels truly authentic? What about it does not?

What parts of you have been lost at work? What are ways to recover these lost parts?

Learning Partner Dialogue

Share the chainsaw armadillos that block you.

Explore similarities and differences in each other's fearful thoughts.

The text reads: "It is in uncovering your wounds that you find the strength to accept the deeper, richer, more vital path of your soul purpose."

Discuss what this mean for you and your work.

Recovering the Lost Parts

You may have been taught from a young age to hide your deepest longings, to deny essential and sacred parts of who you are. In your family, school, and at work you have been encouraged to act as if you are complete while simultaneously exiling valuable aspects of yourself.

"When I was in elementary school," Dianne, a skilled therapist and group leader explained, "my grade was selected to perform at an important community celebration. We were to sing three songs. One day during rehearsal, the music teacher asked me to stop singing. 'You can just mouth the words,' she said, 'but don't sing.' It was humiliating to stand there silently moving my mouth when I wanted to sing."

Your willingness to embrace your wounds leads you to transform your aspirations into reality.

For Dianne this struggle to find her voice and openly express her views went well beyond her elementary school choir. "It is always a challenge for me to speak out," she reflected during a coaching session. "I find myself deferring to those in authority and complaining about it afterwards."

Many people have lost their voices at work. At meetings and during conference calls they sit silent or give half-hearted assent to the ideas of others.

To touch your wounds is to reach out to those neglected parts and to re-incorporate them into your life. They bring you the missing pieces that transform your hopes from strategies for bolstering a false self-image into your true calling. It is in uncovering your wounds that you find the strength to accept the deeper, richer, more vital path of your soul's purpose. By touching those parts of yourself that you had given up for dead, you infuse new life into your work. You find a place of inner authority from which you can lead your work life with authenticity. You begin to dissolve the walls that keep you from fulfilling your calling. You discern more clearly what you are here to contribute.

Start in either place, with your aspiration or your wound. When you look honestly at either, the other one will appear. Your struggle to achieve your aspirations guides you to discover your wounds and your willingness to embrace them leads you to transform your aspirations into reality.

In a Flash of Recognition

Sometimes your calling announces itself in a flash of insight. In the spring of 1970, my colleague Blake Anderson was a college junior slogging through his aerospace engineering major. He was good at the course work, but uninspired. Wandering across campus on April 22 he stumbled into the first Earth Day demonstration. "I stopped in my

> *Disguised as a dull ache or sharp stick prodding you onward, your purpose is trying to get your attention.*

tracks," Blake recounts, "it was an absolute epiphany. I knew then — in an instant — what it was I could give my life to, even though it meant taking extra course work and delaying graduation. I changed my major to environmental engineering, and followed my path."

For Blake, his calling of "fostering the creative coexistence of nature and humanity in complex urban settings" began in that moment. As a policy advisor at the national level and general manager of one of the nation's largest urban sanitation districts, he has consistently followed his calling.

For many people, the realization of their calling is a slower, more exacting process. You catch glimpses and then get sidetracked. You experience the satisfaction of serving a deeper purpose and then you become diverted. You may even forget the real pleasure that comes from following your purpose and become doubtful that it is possible. This is not because you do not have a calling, but because you have not developed a practice that cultivates the quality of attention that can discern that call amid the clamor of everyday life.

In the thrall of the monkey mind you wander off the path of your calling. However, a part of you remembers the way and impels you forward. Disguised as a dull ache or sharp stick prodding you onward, your purpose is trying to get your attention.

To Write or Not to Write

The voice of my true calling has been present in my life from a young age. I have always worshiped at the altar of books. I love books — their look, feel, smell, but mostly their promise. To my soul books represent wisdom. Consequently, I have spent untold hours wandering through bookstores and libraries. I was always searching for that obscure, little-known volume that held jewels of life-enhancing wisdom.

The intensity with which I pursued this quest should have gotten my attention. I could not walk past a used bookstore without going in and combing the shelves.

Unsorted piles of books were particularly compelling, as they offered the most likely place where neglected treasures might be found. In my thirties I became obsessed with the goal of writing a book.

I imagined that writing a book would place me on the same lofty pedestal of wisdom occupied by my literary heroes. I made lists of potential book titles. I filled my journal with possible book concepts. I breathed in the heady fantasy of being a renowned author. And just as quickly exhaled my sense of hopelessness and worthlessness. Who was I to think I had anything wise or new to say? Daily, I see-sawed between possibility and impossibility.

Finally, I started to write my first book. I would go out to the studio in the backyard and sit at my desk. It was time to write, time to be brilliant. Even as my fingertips touched the keyboard, my chainsaw armadillos would begin the attack.

On some mornings I would sit down, fresh from a night's sleep, and boot up the computer. As the manuscript blinked back at me from the screen I would try to think of words to write. My mind would grow numb, my eyelids heavy. Torpor and sluggishness would invade my limbs. I could barely summon the strength to press down on the keyboard. I would fight against the forces that were pulling me downward into my fears — that I know nothing and have nothing to say. I would do jumping jacks before sitting down, hoping that by getting my heart pumping and my blood circulating I could avoid confronting my wounds and just proceed smoothly towards having a New York Times bestseller.

On the Floor

I had to admit I was up against something big when in the middle of a morning's writing session I woke up on the floor of my studio. I had literally fallen over onto the floor, knocked unconscious by my chainsaw armadillos.

It can be terrifying to face your fears and vulnerabilities. Most people will not keel over in broad daylight, but will have other ways of blacking out — turning the light of their awareness from bright to dim, other ways of protecting themselves from experiencing the emotional intensity of their fears.

The pain in these situations stems from having neglected vital parts of yourself for so long. When you block off parts of yourself, you block off the flow of your life. To get your life moving in an authentic direction, you must stop grasping at your hopes and avoiding your fears.

End the War

There is no winner in the internal war between hopes and fears. Regardless of which side wins, your life is lost in the fight, your capacity for high performance and high fulfillment is sacrificed.

I got up off the floor and sat at my desk. I had come to a crossroads. I was in the middle of the battlefield. On one side were my hopes — shining bright and alluring. On the other side, my fears — rusty, unwashed, and dreaded. Everyone arrives here at some point. It is where you choose between perpetuating your inner war or surrendering to a deeper purpose. How you choose determines how you will live, lead, and work. It sets the level of your performance and fulfillment.

Surrender hardly sounds like an act of leadership. Yet the path of surrender is the way beyond the incapacitating polarity of the inner war. At first surrendering can feel like you are dying. What is really ending is the drama of the war that has distracted you for so long. All the noise, turmoil, and activity of that war is dying down. The smoke on the battlefield begins to clear. You discern a path that moves neither in the direction of your hopes nor your fears — but towards your true life.

> There is no winner in the internal war between hopes and fears.

What I had to surrender was both my thirst for literary glory and my dread of being exposed as an intellectual lightweight. To let go of that struggle felt like stepping into the abyss. For years, I had known myself as the person who hoped to write a profound book and the person who fell asleep at the computer. In surrendering the familiar hostilities of my hopes and fears, I felt unprotected and alone.

It was then that the chainsaw armadillos launched their most ferocious attack. With a tidal wave of voices they chided, threatened, and mocked me. Along with the voices came emotions and sensations that coursed through my body like shock waves. My chest tightened, my breath became ragged, I could not focus my eyes. Still I sat there. Though it felt like I was crawling through a dust storm on my hands and knees, I found my way back to the breath. I centered my awareness on the breath, steadied my attention and began to listen to the chainsaw armadillos more closely. I did not push them away and I did not let them carry me away. I sat there and listened.

In the beginning of her magnificent poem, "The Journey," Mary Oliver describes the initial experience of listening to chainsaw armadillos:

One day you finally knew
what you had to do, and began,
though the voices around you
kept shouting
their bad advice —
though the whole house
began to tremble
and you felt the old tug
at your ankles.
"Mend my life!"
each voice cried.

Chainsaw armadillos are full of familiar bad advice. One chorus of my chainsaw armadillos warned me to be careful. They argued in favor of forgetting the whole idea of writing and the dubious possibility of high performance and high fulfillment. "Better to fly under the radar, play it safe, and stick with what you already know how to do," they insisted.

These chainsaw armadillos explained that while over 80,000 books are published each year, most authors make no money for their efforts. Writing a book, they cried, was like inviting failure to take over my life.

Another band of chainsaw armadillos screamed at me for my lackluster efforts. They berated me for slowing down and insisted that I already was a failure considering how few pages I had written. They pointed out all the other people I knew who had written books and exhorted me to get with the program. "Set goals and stick to them. Do it now," they shrieked.

Knots formed and unformed in my stomach as the voices rose and fell. I let my awareness drop beneath the voices to feel the emotions and sensations from which they arose. As I did so the voices of the chainsaw armadillos became softer. A quality of sadness began to envelop my heart. I felt alone. This

> *I let this calling question drop like a pebble into the depths of my mind and listened for an inner response.*

feeling scared me and I automatically began to pull away. But I knew that to stop now would eventually return me to the inner war. Instead I returned to the breath and stopped resisting the feelings of sadness and aloneness. I accepted them. Gradually a sense of warmth began to spread from my heart through my body. I felt at ease, settled, and at peace.

Calming the Lake

In the meditative traditions the mind is often compared to a lake. Any attempt to forcefully smooth the surface of the lake, with hands, paddles, or even wind, only produces more ripples. Only by letting the lake be, by letting the mind be, by establishing an environment of stillness, will the ripples naturally subside. By mindfully accepting the thoughts, emotions, and sensations without suppressing or indulging them, the waves reduce to ripples and the ripples finally rest in stillness.

Then the surface of the lake becomes like a mirror, reflecting without distortion the surrounding trees, hills, even the birds and clouds in the sky. As the mind is stilled, you see the futility of the inner struggle between your hopes and fears.

And when the lake has become calm, you can see into the clear waters and discern that which resides in the very depths. There is a treasure in the depths that is called the pearl of great price in the ancient traditions. It is the final component of your guidance system — your calling.

As I sat on my chair the ripples came. I wanted to be wise. I feared I wasn't. I wanted to write a ground-breaking work that brought me recognition and rewards. I wanted to be as good as my literary heroes, but feared that I wasn't. The waves swelled and subsided. I accepted my feelings of sadness and aloneness. The lake of my mind was still. In that stillness I asked myself what I now refer to as the calling question.

I asked myself, "Through writing this book, *what is it I most deeply want to create?*"

I let this calling question drop like a pebble into the depths of my mind and listened for an inner response. What came back was that *I want to translate the ancient spiritual teachings into words that people can readily understand and use in daily life.*

I dropped the question more deeply, "Through translating spiritual teachings, *what is it I most deeply want to create that is even more important?*" I waited. And gradually I began to hear and feel an answer that felt true. As I sat on my chair the answer that came was *to motivate myself and others to lead inspired lives.*

What was deeper? I asked, *"What is it I most deeply want to create that is even more important to my soul?"* I listened. The answer — *living in the sacred presence.*

There was no denying these answers. They rang true beyond hope and fear. They invited me to live and lead more fully, more widely, more profoundly. It was as though a hand reached out from my heart and clasped the hand of the world. The life within me and the greater life around me greeted one another. All this happened in a matter of minutes. When it was over, I found myself seated in my chair before the computer. The afternoon sun was coming through the window. I began to type.

Mary Oliver describes this passage beautifully through the voices of the chainsaw armadillos into the depths of your own life:

Little by little,
as you left their voices behind,
the stars began to burn
through the sheets of clouds,
and there was a new voice
which you slowly
recognized as your own,
that kept you company
as you strode deeper and deeper
into the world,
determined to do
the only thing you could do —
determined to save
the only life you could save.

The Calling Question

Asking the calling question is one of the most important things you can do to renew and refocus your work. Tell your truth about what matters most to you, even if it sounds impossible, grandiose, or idealistic.

"The place where people meet to seek the highest is holy ground," was the saying above the stage in the auditorium of my elementary school. It has always stuck with me. All work can be holy — a pathway to

> *All work can be holy — a pathway to wholeness, integration, and authenticity.*

wholeness, integration, and authenticity. It is not the task itself but the depth, presence, care, and awareness that you bring to the task. When you seek to follow the directive of your longing through your work, you stand on holy ground and find your path to authentic leadership. The degree to which you hold back from making this connection, is the degree to which you remain caught between your hopes and your fears.

To connect with your calling you simply need to steady your attention, breathe, and ask the calling question. You begin at the surface of the lake focusing on the responsibilities of your current work. This is the starting point. Then, having defined your current work you ask the calling question, *"What do I most deeply want to create through this work?"* This calling question drops, like a pebble, into the lake of the mind and you listen for the answer that arises from within. At first, ripples may appear on the surface. You may feel strange asking yourself the calling question. The simple act of asking it can stir emotions — hopes, fears, desires, and doubts may raise waves on the mind's surface. Allow them to gently subside.

And then ask the question again. This time, let it drop a little deeper. Let the calling question sink further into the lake of the mind and listen as the deeper levels of your being respond. Dropping into the depths of your mind uncovers layers of authentic longing. You discover, as the question sinks in, deeper and deeper answers to the calling question, "What do I most deeply want to create through my work?"

> *Let the question drop inside and just listen for the answer.*

In workshops and retreats, thousands of people have used this process of asking the calling question and listening for the response within. Typically I invite people to work in pairs with one person as the guide and facilitator, asking the question. The other person listens within themselves and gives voice to their deepening answers. The facilitator records the answers for later reference.

One Nurse's Calling

During one of these sessions, I worked with Jeanne at a Nursing Leadership Conference. She had agreed to model the process in front of the group. We sat side by side and I began by explaining, "I'm going to guide you through a process that will help you discover inside yourself the third element of your inner leadership compass — your calling. Are you ready to start?"

Jeanne nodded.

I started by asking about her work. "Tell me about what you do — what you are responsible for."

"Well, I'm a nurse in pediatric oncology," Jeanne explained. "I care for patients, ensure that they have timely and proper medications, and implement protocols."

"So those are your day-to-day tasks. Now, you are going to learn more about the deeper purpose that underlies your work. Shall we begin?"

"Definitely," she responded.

Then, I began to use the calling question in order to help Jeanne move from the task level of her work towards an understanding of the deeper purpose of her calling.

"So Jeanne," I offered, "as I ask you a question listen inside yourself for the answer. Through fulfilling the tasks of patient care, what is it you most deeply want to experience or create?"

Jeanne held her breath for a second, thinking, and then said, "Well, I want to create an environment where every patient gets excellent care."

"Great. Can you sense that answer comes from a deeper place inside you?"

"Yes," she said.

I was ready to ask her the calling question again.

"Let this next question drop even a little deeper. Through creating an environment where every patient gets excellent care, what is it you even more deeply want to experience or create?"

Jeanne looked surprised, "Deeper than patient care?"

"Yes. Let the question drop inside and just listen for the answer."

Jeanne became very still and quiet. She lowered her eyes and went within. When she spoke her voice was soft.

"Yes...there is something deeper," Jeanne whispered. "I want to create an environment where everyone...patients, family, and staff...experiences healing and care."

As Jeanne spoke the quality of attention in the room shifted. People became still. This often happens when one person speaks from the soul. Everyone starts sensing that something real has entered the room. For the person who is speaking dropping deeper feels right, there is a longing to go deeper, and it can be scary. Giving voice to your deeper purpose is not something that is familiar to most people.

I waited a minute before proceeding, "So, Jeanne, let's see what is even deeper. Through creating an environment where everyone experiences healing and care, what do you even more deeply want to experience or create?"

Jeanne was still focused within herself. She let the calling question drop inside. "It sounds almost like too much...but I want to help myself and others fearlessly embrace life and death."

What Jeanne discovered, like thousands of others, is that in the depths of her mind was what the great German poet Goethe called, a "Holy Longing." This longing wants to grow, to give, and to create what matters most. Touching this longing brings light to familiar routines. It reveals that high performance and high fulfillment can come through your work, if you are willing to align your work with your calling.

Dropping the Pebble

Christine, a coaching client, who worked with autistic and developmentally challenged infants, explored the calling question in her journal. She wrote:

> My calling is to experience the beauty and simplicity of supporting a baby to woo her parents into love when they have been frozen in fear. I love figuring out where the sweet spots are that allow a child to give her parents a new look at her strengths, rather than her weaknesses (which brought them to me in the first place). For me (which may sound selfish but is the most important part), the joy is in the discovery, the engagement; being part of a journey that has great importance for the family. This process has deep meaning for me and draws on my creativity in just the right way. The parents see that the baby is already perfect and begin to relate to her in this way...instead of as a project to fix.

There is a simple and uncontrived answer to your calling question. It comes from your soul, from your deep passion and commitment to life. It is not a strategy to get ahead or a slogan to rally the troops. It is simply the calling that you are here to serve.

Reflection & Dialogue: Calling

Personal Reflection

What is your sense of your deeper calling?

Learning Partner Dialogue

In this exercise one person facilitates and asks the questions, while the other simply listens deep inside and answers the questions. Another person can record these answers for later reference.

Stage 1 Start by asking, "What is your current work and what are you responsible for in your job?"

Stage 2 Begin to use the calling question in order to help your learning partner move from the task level of work towards an understanding of the deeper calling. Ask, "Through fulfilling the tasks of ...., what is it you most deeply want to create?" Allow your learning partner the time to reflect and answer.

Stage 3 Keep repeating the process, using the calling question, and inviting your learning partner to listen, feel, and discover what he or she most deeply wants to create through their work.

8

YOUR DHARMA

There is something that...is a great treasure, which
may be called the fulfillment of existence...
The place where this treasure can be found is the
place where one stands...It is here that we should
try to make shine the light of the
hidden divine life.

Martin Buber

We have been exploring the three elements of your inner guidance system:

- Core Values — those deep motivators that are the source of your passion and purpose
- True Gifts — those talents and abilities that are your unique expression of greatness
- Calling — that which you most want to create through your work

Although you discover them one at a time, these three elements — values, gifts, calling — must be integrated into a unified, living whole. Each element is one facet of your authentic leadership. Values provide the ground of inner congruence and integrity. Gifts are the ways that you most powerfully and naturally interact with the world. Calling focuses you in the direction of your soul's longing and purpose.

Writing Your Dharma Statement

Integrating values, gifts, and calling into a unified statement gives form to your inner guidance system. I

119

have helped hundreds of people craft statements that synthesize their values, gifts, and calling into a unified framework. I call these dharma statements. Recall that dharma is that essential function that you are here to express, experience, and fulfill. You realize your dharma when you embody your values, use your gifts, and follow the path of your calling.

Words are powerful. Writing your dharma statement requires thoughtfulness, self-inquiry, and time. Each word counts. Each word is rich with meaning. In the phrasing of your dharma statement, you illuminate your work and define your individual expression of authentic leadership.

Each person's statement is a unique expression of their soul's purpose. One participant in a leadership retreat discovered that her core values were love, freedom, and creativity. Her innate gifts were listening, writing, encouraging, and coaching. Her calling was to bring forth joy, playfulness, and healing in herself and others. She wrote her dharma statement as follows:

To express love, freedom, and creativity through listening, writing, and coaching to bring forth joy, playfulness, and healing in myself and others.

Other seminar participants wrote:

To live my values of peace, growth, and truthfulness using my gifts of organizing, planning, mentoring, and persistence to create systems and technologies that promote a more efficient world that preserves its natural resources.

To live my values of integrity and love through logical reasoning, forthright communication, and creative problem-solving, to build trusting relationships and enduring solutions at work, home, and in the community.

To live with awareness, creativity, and humor and make the complex simple so that people in my city cooperate and prosper.

To embody love, service, and creativity through my gifts of seeing clearly, communicating honestly, and being present to melt fear into love so that children and parents experience each other's perfection and beauty.

Bring the Words to Life

Writing your dharma statement — your personal definition of authentic leadership — is an important step towards achieving high performance and high fulfillment in your work. The words attune your inner guidance system. Reading the statement to yourself and sharing it with others helps internalize the meaning of your values, gift, and calling.

The words of your dharma statement arise from that deeper level of your being. The words strengthen your connection to that deeper level. This is the level of your being that has gently and persistently supported your search for authenticity at work. It is the source of insight, direction, and guidance.

This statement is your dharma. It describes who you are, what you are here for, and how you can best fulfill your leadership destiny. What begins as words starts to live in you. You develop an inner sense that lets you know whether or not you are aligned with your values, using your gifts, and pursuing your calling. Your ability to stay oriented, clear, and balanced strengthens. You start to make real time adjustments that increase your capacity for acting in accord with your values, gifts, and calling.

Reflection & Dialogue: Dharma Statement

Personal Reflection

Review your core values and select three or four of your most important gifts — those that you truly want to use and develop. Then refer back to your answers to the calling question. You answered this question several times. Which of these words captures the calling that you want to devote yourself to at this time?

Craft a dharma statement based on the work you have done so far.

Be creative.

You may need to modify the format in order to make a statement that truly reflects your inner guidance system.

Learning Partner Dialogue

Share your dharma statements with each other. As you read your dharma statement put yourself into the words. Make each word count. As you listen to your learning partners' dharma statements, let yourself feel the life inside the words. Let the words touch your heart.

Talk about what it means to live your values, use your gifts, and follow your calling.

Describe how it feels when you are aligned with your dharma and how you can tell when you are off course.

Identify current situations where it would be beneficial to more fully express your values, use your gifts, and follow your calling. Explore with your learning partners how you might begin to do so.

Celebrate Through Reflection

The ongoing integration of dharma is supported by the practice of reflection. In those situations where you feel congruent, aligned, and satisfied, reflect on how these positive feelings show that you are living your values, using your gifts, and acting in alignment with your calling.

Through reflection you celebrate, expand, and deepen your expression of dharma. It is important to acknowledge the ways in which you are fulfilling your dharma and to notice how this enriches you and your world. It is also important in those situations where you are experiencing discomfort, confusion, conflict, or tension, to reflect on the ways in which you are not living your values, using your gifts, or acting in alignment with your calling. This can be a more challenging, but deeply rewarding reflection.

Transform Yourself

Often when people are unhappy, their tendency is to assume that external conditions are the cause of the dissatisfaction. Other people are *not* behaving as they want them to. Events are *not* proceeding in accordance with plans. People disappoint them and obstacles block their path.

In these situations, people often react and pull back or strike out. They blame others, find fault, complain silently or out loud, all of which serves to reinforce their sense of frustration and certainty that the real problem is "out there" caused and perpetuated by others.

> *The place to begin transforming the situation is within yourself.*

People often overlook their own contributions to the creation of the problem. You are not separate from the situation with which you are unhappy — you are a part of it. When your attention is focused outwardly you see other people and what they are doing. When you are seated around a conference table and the meeting is going poorly, you see other people behaving badly. You don't see yourself — but you, your thoughts, your emotions, what you say and how you say it are part of the meeting. The place to begin transforming the situation is within yourself.

This is the time to use your inner guidance system and give yourself a dharma check-up. You will see ways in which you have deviated from the path of authentic leadership, and recognize which of your core values you need to embody more fully, which of your gifts you need to exercise, and how you can realign with your calling in order to improve the situation.

Your Learning Edge

When you begin to focus within, it becomes clear that all external difficulties have something to teach you. When you look deeply, you see that all challenges bring you to your learning edge, revealing areas within yourself that have not been fully integrated.

On the near side of your learning edge is what you know and have mastered, your well-developed ways of thinking, communicating, and taking action. On the far side of the boundary is uncharted domain. Regardless of its potential, the distant landscape can appear more threatening than inviting. Its malevolent appearance, however, is deceiving.

Your learning edge is the threshold between your past and your possibility. The situations that stymie you the most are those that have the most to offer. Through encountering these situations skillfully you are able to release yourself from limitations and bring untapped gifts to life.

Your learning edge presents a choice as to whether you will move to a new level of performance and a new depth of fulfillment, or persist in the patterns of the past. As you connect to your values, strengthen your gifts, and pursue your calling, challenges are inevitable. You are drawn to them by your own commitment to wholeness. As soon as you realize how much better authenticity works and feels, your inner guidance system will unerringly take you to your learning edge again and again.

No More Delay

Having defined your dharma and brought your inner compass to life, you will find that you cannot live a divided life and leave integral parts of yourself at home when you are at work. When you are divided in this way, you shortchange your life.

Your authenticity cannot be denied. It can only be delayed. When you know your dharma, delaying its implementation creates stress. You realize that true leadership happens now — in the present moment. It happens whenever you live your dharma and support others in being true to theirs.

Learning edges come in different forms. They invite you to step more deeply into life. This might mean making a phone call you have been putting off; talking to your boss about what you really need; accepting responsibility for your contribution to a problem; taking a risk that moves you towards your ideal job; or having a heart-to-heart conversation with someone you have resented.

Poised at your learning edge you may decide to wait

for a better time to step over. Waiting for this better moment can, however, be a long, long, wait. In most of life — in your workplace, family, and relationships — conditions are always in flux. There is always something that could be a little clearer, a little safer, a little more certain.

It is in the midst of life's not-quite-rightness that you step forward to manifest your next level of high performance and high fulfillment. It is within the unsatisfactory and unsettled conditions that you act. The broken nature of the world is your invitation to leadership. You can't wait until you feel more together because this will never happen on the safe side of your learning edge. Although your first steps may be clumsy, without finesse or grace, you step forward nonetheless. It is your own unfinished nature, your own not-quite-rightness with which you act. The incompleteness of the world and your own incompleteness fit each other. Your need for wholeness and the world's need for service complete each other.

Don't Want, Choose

Most people want authenticity, high performance, and high fulfillment. They want to create what matters most to them and experience joy and integrity in the process. But wanting is not the same as choosing.

You can want to improve your work while still remaining passive. If you say, "I want more teamwork with other departments," "I want this conflict to be resolved," or "I want to be more creative at work"

127

without acting then you have not moved across your learning edge from passive wanting to active choosing.

Viktor Frankl was an Austrian psychiatrist imprisoned in the Auschwitz concentration camp for several years during WWII. In those terrible conditions Frankl discovered the power of choice. He wrote, "Everything can be taken away from a man but one thing, the ability to choose one's attitude in a given set of circumstances, to choose one's own way."

Even in a concentration camp, Frankl discovered that he was free to live congruently with his values, to use his gifts, and to choose actions that were noble and meaningful. It is unlikely that anyone reading this book will be imprisoned in a concentration camp.

> Your soul...offers you a compelling vision of what you can create.

But we all face challenges. We all come to our learning edge — to the place where we can choose to hold back or to move forward and act with authenticity.

Your soul has already made its choice. Your soul — the deepest part of you — is waiting for the rest of you to commit. It is like the story of the pilgrim trekking in the Himalayas when the weather turned bitterly cold with harsh winds and pelting rain. Looking out the window at the downpour, an innkeeper asked the pilgrim, "How will you ever get there in this kind of weather?" The traveler answered with a smile, "My heart got there first, so it's easy for the rest of me to follow."

Every time you come to a learning edge, your soul is in the background cheering you on, encouraging you to step over that line into a new level of leadership. Your soul is also far out in front of you, at the horizon line of your awareness, where it offers you a compelling vision of what you can create.

This vision draws you forward and grounds the movement across your learning edge in the soil of reality. Having a vision focuses you on specific results. No longer waiting you know it is time to act. It is time to commit to a vision that you will make real. Your vision may be focused on:

- Transforming your career
- Improving your work-life balance
- Stepping over your learning edge
- Being a better listener
- Being more assertive

This list of possibilities is endless. But your vision very specifically relates to you, to your dharma, and to your work life. The key is to commit to a vision that inspires you to action. Read the words of your dharma statement on a daily basis. Let them sink into your awareness. Feel their significance as you read. Read the words to yourself slowly and let their meaning resonate within you. Allow yourself to reflect on the whole meaning of your dharma statement. Let it inform your vision.

9

CYCLE OF RENEWAL

*The soul's natural movement is not in a straight
line. On the contrary, it circles around a center.*

Plotinus

Your vision draws you forward into action that is now
informed by the knowledge of your dharma and the
feedback of your inner guidance system. The ups and
downs of everyday life become part of a conscious cycle
of renewal, one that continually deepens your ability to
create and enhances your sense of fulfillment in the
process.

This cycle of renewal and learning has definite
phases. As you move through the phases of the cycle you
discover more about what you truly want to create and
in the process unite with the neglected parts of your
soul. You move through the cycle by making conscious
choices that shape your work into a congruent
expression of your core values, gifts, and calling.

All life moves in cycles. Whether you examine a tree
outside your window passing through the cycle of the
seasons or consider the much longer cycle that
constitutes the life of a star, everywhere you look in nature
there are cycles. Nature is the great teacher of renewal.

Realizing your vision and fulfilling your dharma does not occur in a linear fashion. Your growth also follows certain cycles. "To everything there is a season," said the writer of Ecclesiastes. In the busy-ness of your schedule it is easy to lose sight of how life actually unfolds. Marching to the beat of quarterly returns or project plans, you may fall out of step with the unfolding rhythm of your own development.

Inner and Outer Fusion

There is a natural tension between your ability to realize your vision and your degree of congruence with your values, gifts, and calling. The more you are aligned, the more smoothly the cycle proceeds. Obstacles and challenges in the world naturally arise. And although there will be issues to resolve externally, the main focus is on your own inner congruence and clarity. Until you are acting in accordance with your dharma, any action you take will probably exacerbate the problem.

Realizing your vision and fulfilling your dharma does not occur in a linear fashion.

The more you struggle against outer conditions and ignore your own growth, the more road blocks you encounter. Struggle is resolved and obstacles dissolve when you take action while doing the inner work necessary to become the living embodiment of what you seek to create in the world. The more integrated you become, the more you will relax into the unfolding rhythm of the cycle of renewal. Inner work and outer action fuse. As you fulfill each phase of the cycle, you fulfill your dharma — become a whole person and make the contribution that is uniquely yours to offer the world.

Phases of the Cycle

The Cycle of Renewal has four phases — Germinating, Growing, Harvesting, and Transforming. Each phase presents specific rewards and challenges and calls for certain actions and attitudes. Completing these actions and adopting these attitudes moves you through the cycle efficiently and harmoniously (see Appendix).

Following the Cycle of Renewal turns your work life into a conscious ritual. The word *ritual* comes from the Indo-European root *rta,* meaning order. Ritual is the practice of becoming aligned with a larger order. Joseph Campbell, the great interpreter of world mythology, taught that rituals are designed to bring us back into alignment with the rhythm of nature.

There is no set timetable for the unfolding of your dharma. Your cycle unfolds in an orderly fashion but not according to calendar or clock time. Unlike the tree outside your window, which flowers in a particular month each year, the season for realizing your dharma is less predictable. To a large measure, the timing depends on your readiness and willingness to do the work in front of you. The rhythm that the cycle of renewal follows is highly personal and requires your conscious participation in order to progress.

The cadence of the cycle of renewal follows *developmental time* which contrasts sharply with the pace of contemporary life. We live in a nano-second culture where most of us are what author Sue Monk Kidd terms "quick-aholics." We are addicted to the instant response. The practice of patience challenges a mind acclimated to sound bites and instant mashed potatoes. "The soul is the patient part of us," writes psychologist James Hillman. Following the pace of the Cycle of Renewal aligns you to the patient timing of the soul.

Your participation begins by identifying the phase of the cycle you are in. This lets you know where you need to focus and what actions you must take. If you try to skip phases, circumstances will arise that block your forward motion. You must complete the phase you are in before moving on. In realizing your vision and becoming whole, the cycle has its own integrity. Remember, your work life can be in any one of the phases. And if your work life involves multiple roles and responsibilities, each may be at a different phase of the cycle. As you read the descriptions of the phases below, think about where you are now.

Germinating Phase

The cycle begins in the Germinating Phase as you embark on a whole new chapter in your work life. You have let go of the previous cycle and are now drawn towards a new vision of what you want to create. In the Germinating Phase you sense a new direction and your vision is fresh and full of potential. Contemplating the vision fills you with energy. In the Germinating Phase you set the agenda for the next chapter of your work. This is the seeding time, when you are discerning and clarifying the vision that you will create.

Look and Listen

The Germinating Phase starts with simply looking and listening. Looking and listening without preconceptions opens you to discern the new vision that is emerging. Suzuki Roshi, founder of the San Francisco

Zen Center used to tell his students, "In the expert's mind there are few possibilities. In the beginner's mind there are many." You start this phase with the beginner's mind and a sense of open innocence.

In the first part of the Germinating Phase you accept that you don't know exactly what you are going to do next. You're interested, curious, and attentive to the world around you. In the Germinating Phase, you trust that the work you most need to devote yourself to will present itself if you are attentive to what life is asking of you. Your task at this point is to have an open heart and open mind.

> *In the Germinating Phase you are a dreamer and a visionary.*

In the Germinating Phase you are a dreamer and a visionary. With 'beginner's mind' you let the world speak to you. You may talk with people, observe trends, gather data, or study reports. You immerse yourself in the world of possibilities without preconceptions because you recognize that imposing your old assumptions on the current situation will impede your growth and blind you to the vision that is emerging.

Choose and Commit to a Vision

The next task in the Germinating Phase is to choose and commit to a vision. This vision needs to align with your dharma — resonate with your core values, use your gifts, and track with your deeper calling.

This is the time to open up to a vision for work about which you are passionate. The challenge in this phase is to embrace your real vision. In the Germinating Phase you do not need to know how to make the vision real. This is not the time for planning. The key is to be bold and honest. Make sure your vision is an expression of your dharma statement. Author Pearl S. Buck observed, "Once the *what* is decided, the *how* always follows. We must not make the *how* an excuse for not facing and accepting the *what*." This is the time for envisioning what matters most to you and listening to the needs of the world you are called to serve.

Growing Phase

Having chosen a vision you are ready to enter the Growing Phase in which your energy is given to building the dream to make your vision real. Now is the time for action — to set goals, gain needed experiences, build skills, create alliances, enroll others, and build structures and systems to realize your vision. This is the time to set specific objectives, make concrete plans, mobilize needed resources, and take action.

In the Growing Phase you become both a spiritual warrior and a peace maker. You fiercely engage in bringing your vision into form. The sword of the warrior is a symbol of the ability to focus, make distinctions, establish boundaries, and separate true from false. In the Growing Phase you must be decisive and focused. Choosing a vision doesn't mean circumstances will rearrange themselves to make it a reality. Coming face to face with the challenge of making the vision real — is the heart of the Growing Phase.

Connect with Allies and Adversaries

Now is the time to bring in other people and enroll them in your vision. It is time to gather resources; to build systems, structures, and processes that turn ideas into realities.

The sword of the spiritual warrior points both outwardly and inwardly. Because your vision involves and impacts other people, you will inevitably encounter allies and adversaries on the path. It is the adversaries who present the real challenge. How you meet their resistance is central to the successful completion of the Growing Phase.

The key to successfully moving through this resistance is to use it as a mirror in which to view your own imbalances. You listen and learn from other's concerns and use conflict as an opportunity to dialogue and discover new options for collaborative action. In the Growing Phase you are called to engage directly and vulnerably with others. This is where you lay down your sword and act as a peacemaker.

Build Structures and Take Action

The Growing Phase is the season where outer activity is most intense. This intensity moves the vision from concept to reality. If you hold back from engagement you will not complete the work of the Growing Phase. Those who compromise here create half-hearted results with little or no staying power.

This is the time for picking up the sword. Often personal sacrifices have to be made in order to realize your vision. You have to be willing to cut out those old patterns of thought and action that hold you back. The sword of discernment points inwardly. By becoming disciplined and intent on embodying your vision you complete the work of the Growing Phase.

Harvesting Phase

When you have reached the Harvesting Phase, you have established yourself and your vision, built your competency, achieved a level of mastery, and made an impact. You now harvest the results of the vision you chose in the Germinating Phase and the results you created in the Growing Phase.

Sustain Momentum

You should now give your attention to keeping the dream alive as long as it still has meaning. This is the time to be an elder and a mentor, to train others, pass on the torch, guide those who are entering the field, or codify what you have gained in order to pass it on to others.

Review and Evaluate

In the Harvesting Phase you look back to review and evaluate what has been achieved up to this point, reflect on "lessons learned," and acknowledge your accomplishments. This can be a time of celebration and sober reflection. You see in tangible form the ways in which you have stayed true to or lost track of your vision.

The Harvesting Phase prepares you for closing this chapter in your work life. You acknowledge yourself and others for efforts and accomplishments. You honor what has been done and extract lessons from your errors.

At the end of the Harvesting Phase, you know that the cycle has almost run its course. There can be a sense of nostalgia for the past but also an eagerness to go forward. Many people start looking for a new vision at this point. They want to find a new project, endeavor, or goal. But there is one more phase to complete before a new vision can emerge — the Transforming Phase.

Transforming Phase

Nothing lasts forever. As you reach the Transforming Phase it is time to lighten your load. You have now outgrown the beliefs, attitudes, images, structures, and goals that defined your movement through the other three phases. The ways of thinking and working that you have created, cherished, and relied on have stopped making sense.

Not only is the vision that inspired you no longer appropriate — the self that you identified with has become outmoded. This is the time of profound letting go. The task now is to empty the self, without knowing how you will be re-formed or what your vision for the next turn of the cycle will look like.

Be Still

Through letting go, you descend into the depths — into stillness and silence. Only by letting go of the old forms can you make space for something new to be born. This is the most interior phase of the cycle. In spiritual literature it is called the dark night of the soul. Your old ways of staying on track no longer work. You are adrift in an inner sea without stars overhead to guide you. All you can do is let go.

This is the phase when you become a mystic and a shaman. As mystic you let go of the known and the past. You trust in the darkness recognizing that "those who dwell in darkness shall see the light." You become shaman and let the old structure of selfhood be torn apart in full recognition that to hold yourself together at this point of the cycle is to fight with your own destiny. The way forward comes through letting go and surrender.

In the Transforming Phase you shed the layer upon layer of thoughts, beliefs, and habits that you have used to protect yourself from life. These layers have insulated you and comforted you. Now is the time to discard all coverings.

The work of the Transforming Phase is tough. The more you experience not-knowing and uncertainty, the more on course you are. For parts of you that have been successful and acted with certainty, this phase of the cycle feels like death. The forms of knowing and acting that carried you through the past cycle have run their course. They are dying.

Now is not the time for action but for stillness.

Be Receptive

As you let go and release your old identity the stillness deepens. This brings you to the second part of the Transforming Phase where you connect with that which is deepest within you again. You return through the gate of stillness to your dharma. You are infused with a new sense of your values. You connect back to your gifts. You hear your calling afresh.

Completing the Transforming Phase expands your realization of who you are and what your life means. You are ready to begin the cycle again and to discover a new vision for the next chapter of your work.

Wherever you are in the cycle there is specific work to be done. Each phase of the cycle will present you with tests and challenges. By facing these tests and completing the appropriate tasks you liberate the resources that are dormant in your soul and you discover the resources that abundantly surround you in the world.

Reflection & Dialogue: The Cycle of Renewal

Personal Reflection

Where are you now in the Cycle of Renewal?

What is going on?

Which of the tasks for this phase are going well?

Where do you need to put more attention or energy?

Whom do you need to talk with in order to move through this phase?

What elements in your environment are supporting the work of this phase? What elements do you need to adjust or address in order to complete this phase?

Learning Partner Dialogue

Share your reflections regarding the phase of the Cycle you are now experiencing. Ask for feedback from your learning partners regarding their sense of: where you are now in the Cycle of Renewal; which of the tasks for this phase are going well for you; where you need to put more attention or energy; whom you need to talk with in order to move through this phase; the elements in the environment that are supporting your work in this phase; and which elements you need to address to complete this phase.

10

DAWNING OF THE LIGHT

In the sunlight of awareness, each
thought and action becomes sacred.
Thich Nhat Hahn

The keys to creating and recreating your work so that it is deeply rewarding and makes a significant contribution to the world are to:

- Use the inner guidance of your dharma — values, gifts, and calling — to navigate the changing conditions in the world and your organization with high performance and high fulfillment.

- Follow the Cycle of Renewal to convert daily ups and downs into a process of learning and development that integrates inner growth with outer service and excellence.

Attuning to your dharma and following the Cycle of Renewal brings light back to your work. With the dawning of that light, your way forward becomes clear. You no longer deceive yourself into following the paths that lead to burnout, lotus eating, or victimhood. You actively choose high performance and high fulfillment and follow the direction of your inner guidance system.

You stop running from the chainsaw armadillos and instead embrace the fire of the present moment as the perfect time for you to act with passion and purpose. Intertwined with that fire, you watch with appreciation as the outmoded beliefs and assumptions that guided your past decisions turn to ash.

Freed from self-imposed limitations you enter into deeper and more courageous conversations with those at work. You experience the ways in which the organizational culture outside you and the psychological culture inside you mirror each other. That which arises as your external experience offers the ideal conditions for you to cross your learning edge. You smile at the marvelous design of it all.

Life never intrudes but always reflects back what you present.

And with that smile you make an unconditional commitment — to express your values, offer your gifts, and follow your deepest calling. You choose to be an authentic leader — to make your unconditional commitment in the midst of changing conditions. To not wait for the way to be cleared but rather step forward to clear the way for others.

You come to appreciate the ways that life responds to your every move. You see that life never intrudes but always reflects back what you present. Life is ready to support you in high performance and high fulfillment. It only waits for an uncontrived, clear signal from you. In his book *The Scottish Himalayan Expedition,* William H. Murray wrote:

> Concerning all acts of initiative and creation there is one elementary truth, the ignorance of which kills countless ideas and splendid plans: that the moment one definitely commits oneself, then Providence moves too. All sorts of things occur to help one that would never otherwise have occurred. A whole stream of events issues from the decision, raising in one's favor all manner of unforeseen incidents and meetings and material assistance, which no man could have dreamed would have come his way.

Your Leap of Faith

In the climactic scene of the movie *Indiana Jones and the Last Crusade,* Indiana must pass three final tests to reach the Holy Grail and save his dying father. In the first test, called the *Breath of God,* he must bow down at just the right instant to avoid being decapitated by revolving metal blades. In the second test, called the *Word of God,* Jones must walk on just the right stones to spell God's name in Latin and avoid plummeting through the floor to his death. In the final and most challenging test, the *Path of God,* Indiana comes to the ultimate learning edge — a chasm one hundred feet across and a thousand feet deep. On the other side is the door to the Holy Grail. He is told, "Only a leap of faith from the lion's head will prove your worth."

What happens next in the movie defies natural law — Jones is upheld by an invisible force.

Letting go of your past and embracing your possibilities is comparable to Indiana's final trial. Like the hero in the movie, you can choose to take the risk and step forward into thin air. On your journey towards high performance and high fulfillment the invisible force that supports you is your authenticity.

Every moment of life is a moment of truth — a moment for authentic leadership. Life calls to you at every moment and you, by how you live, answer that call. The universe is speaking to you in a million forms — in the form of your co-workers, clients, patients, families, and friends; in the form of flowers, trees, and coffee mugs. In every experience you have, life asks if you are willing to experience high performance and high fulfillment.

Listen right now for your answer. If you listen mindfully you will hear, deeper than thought, the voice of your dharma, your inner guidance system. There is a living force field within your soul that gently and persistently supports your search for high performance and high fulfillment. Your inner guidance system is linked to a living state of consciousness within you that knows your path to greater creativity and meaning at work. When you are in touch with this state of consciousness, you naturally make choices and take actions that generate high performance and high fulfillment. You dissolve all hesitancy and open to that which you are here to realize.

When you commit to live authentically, your life becomes an offering. You put your energies, your thoughts, your emotions, and your internal and external actions into the service of life. Transcending selfishness and unselfishness, you do what you have come to do. The laws of nature support and encourage your actions. The question of whether you are ready and willing to experience high performance and high fulfillment is answered, not theoretically, but as a living reality.

You have become a blessing to yourself and to the world.

****

APPENDIX

Wherever you are in the Cycle of Renewal there are key tasks to complete. Use the following guidelines and suggestions to support you in doing the work of the phase you are experiencing.

Tools for the Germinating Phase

You have two things to do in the Germinating Phase. One is to be open to the vision that is taking shape within you and to the changes that are happening around you. The other is to clearly state your intention about what you want to create in this new career cycle. This does not necessarily mean changing your outer situation. It does mean taking responsibility for bringing more of your values and gifts to your work and aligning your new vision with your calling. In short, making this new turn of the cycle a more congruent expression of your dharma statement.

To move through the Germinating Phase consider the following questions:

Look & Listen: Paying Attention Inside & Outside

1. When you think about this new chapter in your career, what ideas and images are active in your mind?

2. When you listen to your core values, what do they tell you is important to remember as you move into this new chapter of your career?

3. What are the major trends/changes impacting your job/team/organization?

Choose and Commit to a Vision. Focus on the vision that you want to create. Focus on what you want, not the means to get there, nor how you will do it.

1. What I want to create is...

2. In what ways does this vision align with your values, gifts, and desired calling?

3. What about the vision is still unclear? How can you make it clearer? Who can help you?

List areas for development and learning

Now that you have your vision clarified, list two or three areas for learning and development that will be key to your vision. These may be specific competencies you want to improve, areas you want more experience in or exposure to, experiences that will "stretch" you into better alignment with your values, opportunities to have a more purposeful impact.

Have feedback conversations

An important next step is to have conversations with a trusted colleague, an organizational leader (ideally your immediate supervisor), and a mentor. These conversations are about your vision and the areas for development and learning you want to focus on.

These conversations can be a time to:
- Get feedback on how your vision fits with organizational realities
- Get support for pursuing what you want

Whom I will talk to:

When I will talk with them:

Tools for the Growing Phase

You have two areas of focus in the Growing Phase. It is time to make your vision real, which means building the systems, structures, and processes that can realize the dream. It is about taking action and getting very specific. The other key task of this phase is to bring in other people to find support and coaching, and to take advantage of organizational and professional resources.

This can be a challenging time; but remember, the biggest obstacles are inside you. They come in the form of your own doubts, fears, and frustrations. These kind of blocking thoughts and emotions are normal. Be gentle with yourself. Don't buy into your own negative chainsaw armadillos. Find methods that help you reaffirm your dharma and stay motivated. To create your action plan for completing the Growing Phase, consider the following questions:

Build Systems and Take Action

1. What kinds of structures can you create that will help make your vision real? (Examples include: building a timeline, creating a strategy and defining intermediary goals, enrolling in educational programs, becoming a member of a professional association, starting a coaching relationship, etc.)

2. What organizational resources can you identify to help make your vision real? (Examples include: your immediate supervisor, training and development programs, job postings, career resource centers, Web sites, etc.)

3. What will keep you motivated to take action, particularly when things get tough or slow down?

Connect with Allies and Adversaries

1. What people can give you the kind of support, feedback, and advice you need to make your vision real?

2. Who opposes your plan or has doubts about your goals?

3. What do you need to do to build relationships with them, learn about their legitimate concerns, and open up communication?

Set Goals

With answers to the above questions, it's time to set three to five goals. By achieving these goals you will be taking concrete steps to make your career vision real.

Your goals should follow the SMART goals format. SMART is an acronym that means:

• **Specific:** Make your goals specific enough that anyone who reads them will know what you mean. "Become a better communicator" is too general. "Be able to give difficult feedback in a direct and caring manner" — that's specific.

• **Measurable:** How are you going to know that you've achieved success in attaining your goal? If you are wanting to master a skill how will you be able to measure your improvement? For any goal it is possible to devise a measurement of success.

• **Attainable:** The goals you set should be challenging. They should feel difficult and at the same time compelling. Define the goal so that achieving it will be a worthy "stretch" of your abilities. The goal should inspire you enough to move you out of your comfort zone.

• **Relevant:** How relevant is the goal to your values, gifts, and desired impact? If it is not a real fit with your High Performance/High Fulfillment prescription, it may not be what you really want. Another aspect of relevance is how the goal fits into the organizational context. Seek out a trusted leader to find out if your goals are relevant to the organization.

• **Time-bound:** It is important to have target dates to work towards. By when will you complete the class, get the certification, meet with your coach, complete the project?

Determine Sub-Goals

For each goal set a number of intermediary or sub-goals. These are like stepping stones that naturally lead to your chosen destination.

Identify the resources you need

As you examine the goals and sub-goals consider what resources you will need in order to be successful. In general these resources will come from within yourself, from other people, from the organizational system, or from some system outside the organization.

Tools for the Harvesting Phase

You have two main areas of focus in the Harvesting Phase. One is to sustain the momentum of the work you are doing. Attention should be given to keeping the dream alive as long as it still means something to you and serves a valuable purpose. The other task is to review and celebrate what has been achieved up to this point. Take time to record "lessons learned" and acknowledge accomplishments. Extend the blessings of your accomplishments to others. This can be time to become a mentor and coach to others who want to learn what you have mastered. To create your action plan and complete the Harvesting Phase consider the following questions:

Sustain Momentum

1. What actions can be taken to sustain your momentum at this point?

2. What achievements should be acknowledged and celebrated?

3. Are there individuals or teams that deserve special recognition for their contribution?

4. How can you share the results of your efforts with

others in order to maintain organizational support? (Examples include: special presentations, meetings, article in organization's newsletter, etc)

Review and Evaluate

1. What is working well?
2. What needs improvement?
3. How satisfied are the customers/beneficiaries of your work efforts? (use interviews, satisfaction surveys, etc)
4. What have you learned?
5. What would you do differently next time?
6. How can these lessons be documented for the future?

Set Goals

Given your answers to the above questions, it's time to set three to five goals. By achieving these goals you will be taking concrete steps to complete the work of this phase. Your goals should follow the SMART goals format outlined on page 155.

Determine Sub-Goals

For each goal set a number of intermediary or sub-goals. These are like stepping stones that naturally lead to your chosen destination.

Identify the resources you need

As you examine the goals and sub-goals consider what resources you will need in order to be successful. In general these resources will come from within yourself, from other people, from the organizational system, or from some system outside the organization.

Tools for the Transforming Phase

You have two main areas of focus in the Transforming Phase. The first task is to let go of the past. By letting go of the old forms, structures, and perspectives, you free yourself from the pull of the past. Take some time to be still and rest. Some of the most important work of this phase occurs when you give yourself time and space to simply be, not to do. Just to be still and let the natural rejuvenating powers of your body and mind work their silent magic. Then it is time to move on. This is an active acknowledgement and appreciation of the past cycle as you open to the new one that is waiting to be born.

To create your action plan for completing the Transforming Phase consider the following questions:

Let Go

1. What behaviors and habits is it time to let go of?
2. What situations, relationships, and projects do you need to let go of?
3. What attitudes about yourself have outlived their usefulness?
4. What realizations, techniques, or people can help you through the letting go process?
5. What thoughts or feelings make it hard for you to let go?

6. What will help you let go of those?

Be Still and Receptive

1. How can you make time for your mind and body to rest? (list at least three ways)

2. What places, people, and practices will be rejuvenating for you at this time?

3. What thoughts or feelings could make it hard for you to take time to be still?

4. How can you work with those so that you do take time?

Next Steps

Given your answers to the above questions, it's time to set three to five goals — even if these are "goals" for being still. By meeting these goals you will be taking concrete steps to complete the work of this phase.

Personal Practices

• Personal practices/techniques I will use to let go are:

• Personal practices/techniques I will use to be still, rest, and rejuvenate are:

• People I will talk with to get support in letting go and being still are:

Make Time and Space

• I will use my letting go practices/techniques at these times/places:

• My rest and rejuvenation "being still" schedule will include:

Products and Services

Now that you've read *You Are the Leader You've Been Waiting For,* you will want to reinforce what you've learned by teaching others and by having products that support your learning just an arm's reach away. Bulk quantities of the book as well as the following products can be ordered at www.dharmaconsulting.com.

To learn more about the products and services visit www.dharmaconsulting.com or please call Eric Klein at 760-436-5535.

Workbook

This companion to *You Are the Leader You've Been Waiting For* provides structured exercises and additional hands-on material for enjoying high performance and high fulfillment at work.

Audio Recording

Read by the author. An ideal way to reinforce your learning as you commute, exercise, or travel.

Video/DVD

Recording of Eric teaching the principles and methods of the book. Helps initiate lively discussions with team members, colleagues, fellow volunteers, family members, and other groups.

Guided Meditation CDs

Eric has taught hundreds of people how to meditate. These recordings bring his teachings to you in an easy-to-use format. Comes with workbook.

Discover Your Gifts Assessment
Use the Elements of Personality Assessment to better understand your gifts and strengthen your ability to use your innate talents creatively.

Identify Your Core Values Cards
This interactive tool will help you and your colleagues and family members identify their core values — the source of passion and purpose within. Thousands of people in organizations around the world have benefited from this enjoyable tool.

Leadership Seminar
Customized workbooks, trainers' guides, and job aids.

Newsletter
Free quarterly e-newsletter full of practical tips and techniques as well as inspiring stories to enhance your leadership and enrich your life. Subscribe online at www.dharmaconsulting.com.

Services

Eric Klein is available for any of the following:

Keynote Speaking to associations, corporations, foundations, and other groups who want to change, grow, and ignite new levels of leadership.

Coaching for personal, professional, and/or spiritual development. Intensive one-on-one work with Eric for those who want greater focus, depth, and meaning in work and life.

Team retreats for leaders and colleagues who want to accelerate change and accountability.

Culture Change Solutions for organizations that want high levels of alignment and collaboration in order to create business breakthroughs.

Spiritual Retreats for individuals wanting to deepen their spiritual lives and explore how to live more mindfully and intentionally in daily life.

Workshops to experience *You Are the Leader You've Been Waiting For* as an interactive seminar.

"Train the trainer" programs designed to teach in-house leadership development specialists how to deliver Eric's leadership workshops.

To book Eric Klein as a Keynote Speaker for your next event call (760) 436-5535.

Contact information:

Dharma Consulting
1455 Hymettus Ave.
Encinitas, CA 92024
760 – 436-5535
email: info@dharmaconsulting.com
www.dharmaconsulting.com

Eric is interested in hearing from you regarding:

- How you have applied *You Are the Leader You've Been Waiting For* in your career or workplace

- Stories of your experiences with this material

- Questions regarding *You Are the Leader You've Been Waiting For*

- Challenges you are facing in making *You Are the Leader You've Been Waiting For* work for you

Please contact Eric at eric@dharmaconsulting.com

To Do or Not To Do:
How Successful Leaders
Make Better Decisions

by Gary Winters & Eric Klein

This quick-read parable lies in a sweet spot between Blanchard and Drucker — engaging story-telling that is also sufficiently prescriptive to give leaders direct guidance on handling real-world situations. All good managers want to empower their people, but it's never easy to know just when to share power, and when to pull it back. This book shows you how.

To Do or Not To Do is sure to help all leaders make better decisions. Don't miss it! – Ken Blanchard, coauthor, *The One Minute Manager.*

$18.95 from www.ToDoBook.com or 760-436-5535